The Other Side of the Tapestry

The Other Side of the Tapestry

Choosing to Trust God When Life Hurts

Maureen Longnecker

WinePress Publishing (PO Box 428, Enumclaw, WA 98022) functions only as book publisher. As such, the ultimate design, content, editorial accuracy, and views expressed or implied in this work are those of the author.

ISBN 13: 978-1-4141-2245-8
ISBN 10: 1-4141-2245-4
Library of Congress Catalog Card Number: 2011960232

To God—I could never thank You enough for all You've done for me
To my husband, Eric—I love, appreciate,
and respect you more than you'll ever know
To my children: Benjamin and Whitney, Daniel, and Naomi—
Each of you is a precious gift from God
To my brother, Jimmy—I'm glad I still have you

In memory of
Jim and Milly Maier
and
Charles and Dorothy Longnecker

Contents

The Weaver

My life is but a weaving
Between my Lord and me,
I cannot choose the colors
He worketh steadily.

Oft times He weaveth sorrow,
And I, in foolish pride
Forget He sees the upper
And I, the underside.

Not till the loom is silent
And the shuttles cease to fly
Shall God unroll the canvas
And explain the reason why.

The dark threads are as needful
In the Weaver's skillful hand
As the threads of gold and silver
In the pattern He has planned.

—Benjamin Malachi Franklin (1882–1965)

Acknowledgments

With special thanks—

to the members and attendees of West Side Baptist/Journey Christian Church (1985–present) for ministering God's love to our family

to Tony and Carol Cassara, John and Lin Lohman, Gregg and Sue Terry, and Jeff and Lisa Wood for the part you have played in our lives, and for the blessing of your friendship

to John Lohman for helping me out of the black hole of depression

to Nathan Longnecker for your compassionate heart and listening ear

to Bruce McMichael for your unique blend of professionalism and compassion

to Uncle Bill and Aunt Mary Moore for your love and support in our shared loss to Bob Page for the hours you put into wordsmithing the manuscript

to Ryan and Bethany Terry for your technical expertise and creativity with the cover photo

to Sharon Wittke for telling me about Jesus

to Jeff Wood for always being there for Eric

to my phenomenal critique team: Kelly Fasoldt, Krista Monroe, Bob Page, and Jenn Wood for giving up your time to read the manuscript, and for your invaluable insights and input

"May the LORD repay you for what you have done. May you be richly rewarded by the LORD . . . ."

—Ruth 2:12

Chapter 1

Dropping into a Black Hole

"MOM, I NEED you to pray for me," my then-teenage son, Benjamin, said as he entered the kitchen.

"Sure. What do you want me to pray for?"

"I'm angry with God."

Thankfully, I didn't react as I might have in previous years, when I would have felt compelled to hold him captive in conversation and quote verses at him until he said he no longer felt that way.

"If I had been God," he continued, "I would have squashed sin like a bug right in the Garden of Eden, and that would have been the end of it. Then we wouldn't have all the problems sin brings. Why did He have to create the Tree of Knowledge of Good and Evil and allow the possibility for sin to enter the world? Why did He allow Satan to sin and fall from heaven? I don't understand why God allowed sin to occur in the first place."

Before I tried to answer his questions, I knew I needed to address a vital truth he had touched on without knowing.

"Benjamin, I'm going to tell you something that I didn't understand until after Papa's death. It's one of the most important truths I've learned in my Christian life."

I locked eyes with my son, wishing I had the ability to instantaneously bestow on him a depth of understanding that I knew only comes from experience. My own understanding of what I was about to say had come as a result of having gone through much heartache.

"Benjamin," I began, "there are many times when we don't get answers to our questions, especially the 'why' questions in this life. At times like that, we're left with a choice. We can allow our questions to turn into mistrust of God and His Word. Or, we can hang onto the truth about God's character as revealed in His Word, even when life doesn't make sense.

"Continue to be honest in your relationship with the Lord. Keep asking hard questions, but you also need to accept the fact that you aren't going to get all your answers on this side of eternity. Don't allow the unanswered questions and the unfulfilled desire for understanding get between you and God."

I can identify with Benjamin's plight that day. The older I become, the more unanswered questions I have. Life's events haven't played out the way I thought they were going to. I never would have guessed that the close-knit, loving family I grew up in would be tragically ripped apart before I was out of my thirties, or that my adult life would include so many painful events. Life doesn't always work out the way we want it to or the way we thought it would, does it? Sometimes we think we know how a situation will turn out, only to have it transpire very differently.

Take Mary, for instance. The circumstances surrounding her giving birth made for quite an experience, but not the kind I would have anticipated if I'd been in her place. If I was almost ready to deliver a baby and was told I must travel to my husband's hometown on foot or on the back of a smelly animal, I'd probably think, *I didn't sign up for this!*

A required journey, no housing accommodations, and giving birth in a manger aren't the kinds of details I would want to write in my son's baby book.

Similarly, many of the events I share in this book were not my choices. Many times I longed for God to miraculously deliver me from circumstances I faced. I don't like the pain, uncertainty, changes, and lack of normalcy that are characteristic of trials.

Thankfully, God doesn't waste opportunities to teach us more about Himself as we go through painful experiences.

Psalm 73:26, 28 says, "My flesh and my heart may fail, but God is the strength of my heart and my portion forever . . . . But as for me, it is good to be near God. I have made the Sovereign LORD my refuge; I will tell of all your deeds."

Those verses capture the reason for this book. I want to tell others what God has done for me, so they can see His loving faithfulness in action. He's taken me through a number of painful, life-changing experiences. In the process, He's taught me to value His person and presence above all else.

Looking back, I can see how He began early to prepare me for what He knew I would eventually face. As a teenager, a poster on my bedroom wall quoted an unknown author who said: "The highest pinnacle of the spiritual life is not happy joy in unbroken sunshine, but absolute and undoubting trust in the love of God."

I kept the poster because I liked the picture on it. The quotation perplexed me, because I sensed a deeper meaning in the words than I had realized. I understood the words grammatically, but not spiritually.

I believe God embedded those words in my heart because He knew I was going to face painful circumstances that would threaten to undermine my faith in His love. He also knew that by clinging to the biblical truth they convey, I would come to understand their deeper meaning.

One of the first trials I faced as an adult was a major depression that lasted about two years. My husband, Eric, and I were living in an apartment on the campus of Washington Bible College (WBC) in Lanham, Maryland, when it started. I had one semester left to finish my bachelor's degree, and we thought it would be a breeze. What we didn't factor into the equation was a rough pregnancy beginning a month and a half after we were married or the hormonal imbalance and the ensuing depression it caused.

My first indication that something was emotionally out of kilter happened one night as I listened to an ice hockey game on the radio while waiting for Eric to get home from work. When I heard an advertisement for Whirlpool that said, "so much to do and only one of you," I had an uncomfortable feeling of pressure inside me. I thought it odd, but brushed it off.

When it happened every time I heard the ad, I realized something was wrong. Not knowing what it was, I avoided it by turning the radio off during ads.

Our son, Benjamin James, joined us in the spring of 1985. Between trying to finish my class work and taking care of Benjamin, I had limited time to deal with the strange feelings that accompanied the depression. I tried to ignore them, but they only got worse as my unidentified hormonal imbalance continued unchecked.

That fall, we moved to Rochester, New York, to go through a one-year missionary internship at West Side Baptist Church (now Journey Christian Church). Eric and I each had been heading for career missions from an early age—Eric since third grade, and I since seventh grade. We were high school sweethearts who had already taken many intentional steps toward our goal by the time we arrived at West Side.

In looking back, I realize we were young and not as mature as we thought we were. Our years of focused preparation had been beneficial, but they also had given rise to an unhealthy self-confidence in our abilities. We sincerely wanted to serve God, but our focus was on what we wanted to do for Him instead of on His desire to use us to accomplish His plans and purposes (Philippians 2:13). We didn't recognize it for what it was: pride.

God had much more in mind for us than just missionary training when He led us to West Side. We needed to learn about grace and humility. To do that required a unique and amazing family of believers, and that is what we found.

On October 1, 1985, we loaded a U-Haul truck to make the move from Pennsylvania to Rochester. The truck and driver were provided by West Side. When we arrived, a group of Westsiders were waiting to unload the van. They moved our belongings into a two-bedroom apartment that had been handpicked for us by Tony and Carol Cassara, a young couple on the missions committee. We found some basic groceries in the refrigerator, a homemade dessert on the counter, and many bags of nonperishable food they had collected by having a church-wide food shower for us!

After everything was unloaded, Tony and Carol asked if we would like to stay at their home for the night because our carpet was damp from cleaning and there was an odor of fresh paint. We took them up on their offer and enjoyed beginning to know them. It would mark the start of a close relationship for our families.

West Side was the perfect environment for us to grow and develop in the way we needed to. They accepted us, invested their time in our lives, and taught us how to follow Jesus' model of grace. They taught us how the church is supposed to function by walking with us through the uninvited trials that would come. West Side was also God's provision for me to get the help I needed.

After we settled into our new routine, it didn't take long for my internal storm clouds to leave their position on the horizon and engulf me with an emotional torrent unlike anything I had experienced.

The depression dropped me into a black hole. Daily, waves of intense feelings of hopelessness washed over me and threatened to overwhelm me emotionally. I often paced our apartment feeling like a trapped animal, powerless to free myself from my invisible cage. Sometimes I paused at the dining-room window and stared at nearby apartment buildings. I wondered if anyone in them was going through the same nightmare.

It got to the point that I believed that Eric would be better off with a different wife and Benjamin would be better off with a different mother. When thoughts of suicide occasionally passed through my mind, subtly suggesting suicide as the only way out of the pain, I knew I needed help.

I began weekly counseling sessions with John Lohman, the Pastor of Family Life and Counseling at West Side. He tested me and Eric and discovered we were both clinically depressed, mine was severe and Eric's was moderate. Then we each took a personality inventory and found that we both needed a lot of work in the area of perfectionism. No surprise there! Our strict background fed into our perfectionistic outlook and the self-imposed, unattainable demands we placed upon ourselves.

While neither of us had been consciously aware of marital problems, our conversations in John's office brought areas of needed improvement to the surface. I was astonished that issues kept popping up.

We learned we had different ways of expressing and receiving love. Eric showed his love by doing things for me. I wanted him to take a break, sit down, and listen to me!

I wanted to hear about Eric's day as soon as he came home, but he needed space for some downtime before he was ready to talk. When he finally did talk, he gave me the "man's version" of his day. I wanted the "woman's version." I didn't know that men and women were created so differently.

Eric kept a mental list of chores to complete. Although I can read, I can't read a list inside someone's head, especially when I don't know it's there in the first place! Eric would come home to find I had worked on jobs that were low on his list of priorities and be disappointed I hadn't done what he felt were the most important chores. I'd be devastated that he was upset with me and felt as if he didn't appreciate what I did accomplish. What a mess!

One by one, John helped us work through sensitive areas. He taught us practical methods to use in dealing with relational problems and how to build a strong, healthy marriage. We read about the primary love languages people have and began to understand where each other was coming from. We realized we needed to "date" by setting aside time to do something together besides work. We started to appreciate each other again and not take our relationship for granted.

Our communication improved, and our awareness of potential problem areas heightened. John taught us how to respect the other person's style of communication instead of each of us expecting our own style to be the only one we used in our marriage. As he worked with us, he equipped us with a "tool box" we could use for the rest of our lives.

As our counseling sessions progressed, John recognized that I needed medical intervention as well as continued counseling. He advised me to consult a psychiatrist to see if I would benefit from an antidepressant.

I initially balked at his advice, even though the depression negatively affected every area of my life. I had preconceived ideas and assumptions that I needed to examine first. My view of depression and my pride were two areas I had to address.

I had an improper view of depression—and the use of medication—that was rooted in my acceptance of the counsel I'd received during my freshman year of college.

When I had gone home for Christmas break, my mom was suffering from a severe depression. Not having experience with treating depression, my dad and I asked for advice. I can still recall what took place one afternoon.

Mom was sitting at the table. Her shoulders rose and fell in jagged motions as she tried to contain her muffled sobs. I stared at her back helplessly, not knowing what to do. I had never seen anyone cry as much as she had the past few days I had been home.

I turned to her pastor, who was leaning against the kitchen counter next to me, and softly asked, "Well, what do you think?"

He shook his head and said, "I don't know what the matter is. It must be unconfessed sin in her life. I don't know what else it could be."

Mom's anguished wail pierced the air in response to his words. "No! It's not sin!" She dropped her head and a shudder rippled through her body. She shook uncontrollably and choked out her plea, *Oh, dear Lord, please help me! He thinks it's sin! You know it isn't, Lord! Oh, God, please help me! Please help me!*

That was my first experience with depression.

Four years later I experienced my own struggle with it. I came to know how it felt, and found that no matter how hard I tried, I could not will it away, pray it away, or release myself from its painful grip.

In addition to the depression itself, I wrestled with troubling questions: *Why is there a stigma in Christian circles about depression? Why do some Christians equate depression with sin? What if they're right? Where does that leave me in God's sight? Have I let Him down? Is He disappointed with me? Is He angry with me?*

I knew that many people who tie depression with sin also believe that taking an antidepressant is wrong.

John didn't hold that view. He explained that because we are fearfully and wonderfully made, a slight imbalance or abnormality in our body's God-created design can wreak havoc on our health. Just as a person with diabetes might require insulin to regulate his or her blood sugar, so a person with depression might require an antidepressant to correct a chemical or hormonal imbalance.

While that made sense, I had a lingering fear that I would let God down if I took an antidepressant, because I knew my mother's pastor disagreed with its use. It's hard to do something when someone you deeply respect thinks it's wrong, especially when that someone is a minister. I respected John, but I also respected Mom's pastor.

Pride also held me back. I'm ashamed to admit that I felt that way, but I was afraid people at church would think less of me if they knew I took an antidepressant.

I asked God to miraculously take the depression away. I begged. He had other plans.

He reminded me of how Jesus healed a blind man one day (John 9). Instead of instantly healing him with a spoken word or a touch, Jesus did something unusual. He spit on the ground and made mud. Then He put the mud on the blind man's eyes and told him to wash it off in a specific pool on the other side of town. The man did what Jesus told him to do, and he received his sight.

Then there was Naaman, the leprous Syrian captain, who expected Elisha to call on God to heal him. When Elisha sent a messenger to tell Naaman to go wash himself in the Jordan River seven times, Naaman became angry and wasn't going to do it. If his servants hadn't talked him into doing it, he wouldn't have been healed (2 Kings 5).

I realized that God doesn't always choose to heal instantly. Sometimes a person needs to take action in order to become well.

I decided to take John's advice. I'm glad I did, because he was correct in thinking I needed medical intervention. Taking an antidepressant proved to be an important factor in my journey toward wellness.

I thank God for giving men and women the ability to make the medication I take. Off medication, the tumultuous emotional rollercoaster begins again. On medication, I'm able to be myself. For that, I am truly thankful.

I also thank God for giving me a pastor who understood my need for medical intervention and who guided me in taking the action I needed to take.

Like my mother and me, many people turn to ministers for advice. Unfortunately, respect for the position of a minister can lead people to accept misleading counsel as godly and true, simply because a spiritual leader gave it. If the one giving counsel doesn't understand clinical depression and rejects the potential benefits of medication, his or her counsel is dangerous at its best—lethal at its worst.

One pastor I spoke with advises people not to take antidepressants. He says that in the absence of a documentable organic cause such as an underactive thyroid, the Bible contains everything needed to overcome depression. This advice assumes that medical science has already discovered everything there is to learn about what causes depression and that every cause is documentable using current technology. It also means that some people who need medication are being told they shouldn't take antidepressants.

John included biblical principles and promises in our sessions. They were a necessary and helpful part of my treatment, but in and of themselves they did not touch my hormonal imbalance. I needed medication to correct that.

Sadly, people who put a high priority on trying to live in a God-honoring way are often the ones who fall prey to this incorrect teaching about antidepressants. Their desire to do what God wants them to do puts them in a tough situation when they know something is wrong with their bodies, but are told a viable treatment option is sinful. Rather than risk doing something that might be wrong in God's eyes, many suffer the consequences of living with untreated depression.

My friend fell into this trap. She called me one morning, and my heart sank when I heard her quivering voice. She was an emotional wreck. She hadn't slept at all that night and asked if I could drive her to a counseling appointment that morning.

I wondered what had happened to her. I knew she had previously struggled with depression, but medication had enabled her to get back to her normal self.

She said, "I went off my medication. I did it with my doctor's permission. I wanted to see how I would be if I was off it."

Why did she do that? I thought she had this settled. It didn't make sense.

As if she knew what I was thinking, she said, "I listened to another one of *those* sermons, and I was afraid I was letting the Lord down."

I was sad, frustrated, and angry. I was sad that my friend was once again dealing with the horrendous pain of depression. I was frustrated by the knowledge that her suffering was unnecessary, and I was angry that some ministers wreak havoc in people's lives by continuing to treat medical matters as though they are spiritual shortcomings.

I'm thankful every time I hear a preacher tackle this topic and give an accurate portrayal of clinical depression. People need to be emotionally freed up to shamelessly pursue medical help when it's needed.

Be careful about who you turn to for advice. Selecting a counselor calls for the same kind of careful discernment as choosing a physician. We all have capability limitations. Choose help from those who recognize their own.

By the way, years after that day in the kitchen, my mother's pastor began taking an antidepressant on the advice of his physician. He was pleasantly surprised at the positive changes it made in his daily life. His willingness to change his opinion, view clinical depression as a medical issue, and accept the use of antidepressants when warranted gives me hope that others will do the same.

Chapter 2

Coming Up from the Bottom

HEBREWS 11 CONTAINS what is often called the "Faith Hall of Fame." It lists people who faced trials and commends them for their faith. In the beginning of the chapter, the writer names men who accomplished feats through faith such as shutting lions' mouths, conquering kingdoms, and routing armies.

We love to read about God divinely intervening and delivering His own. That's the type of action we would like to see from Him all the time.

The passage goes on to tell us what happened to the other heroes of faith. Theirs is a radically different story. They were tortured, jeered, flogged, chained, imprisoned, stoned, sawed in half, and killed by the sword.

Any elation at the start of the text plummets considerably at the brutal reality of what happened to the rest of them.

Hebrews 11:39–40 says, "These were all commended for their faith, yet none of them received what had been promised. God had planned something better for us so that only together with us would they be made perfect."

Stop and consider what those verses tell us. In the midst of the horrific, God had a plan. Not only did He have a plan, but it also included us.

Hang on to that truth tightly, because it's a foundational cornerstone for our lives as we face difficult circumstances that are beyond our control and understanding. God is sovereign over all, and He is working out His plan and purposes, even when it seems as if our world is falling apart. Allow that truth to take root in your heart and to grow deep. It will help you when the pain of a trial threatens to erode your confidence in God.

With Mom's experience as my only previous experience with depression, I had a lot to learn during my own battle.

Psalm 8:3–4 says, "When I consider your heavens, the work of your fingers, the moon and the stars, which you have set in place, what is man that you are mindful of him, the son of man that you care for him?" The Creator of this universe holds all power in His hands. He also loves us individually, and has initiated an eternal love relationship with us.

In the darkness of my depression, I learned more about God's love. Stripped of my normal abilities in many areas, I experienced His unconditional love apart from anything I did. His love does not depend on my "performance."

I also learned some simple but effective strategies for coping with trials. Intentionally focusing on the basics helps counteract the sense of drifting helplessly and aimlessly.

Maintaining as much routine as possible provides a measure of normalcy. It doesn't change the fact that there are many loose ends that need attention, but it does serve as a solid framework from which to build.

Good sleep and proper nutrition (or not), affect our outlook and ability to face the day. God created our bodies out of the dust of the earth (Genesis 3:19). He knows how frail we are. Sometimes we don't recognize our own frailty, and we drive our bodies to function in ways they aren't designed to perform. Then we wonder why we feel the way we do. We shouldn't wonder when it's the result of mistreating our bodies. Along with proper rest and nutrition, we need exercise. It doesn't have to be elaborate, expensive, or demand tremendous exertion. Something as simple as going for a walk has positive effects.

Sometimes we are tempted to "hole up" and avoid interacting with others, especially when we are depressed. While understandable, it isn't good. We need to connect with someone in meaningful conversation for at least five minutes every day. Children, sleeping spouses, and pets don't count.

In addition to spending time with others, we need to spend time with God. I know it can be challenging to read His Word and pray on a daily basis. We can hit dry spells, and our shriveled spirits don't find refreshment in the Word, so we don't see the value of it. We can't find a quiet place to concentrate. When we finally do sit down, someone or something interrupts us before we get our eyes closed or the Bible open. The obstacles are never-ending, but so is our need for maintaining a close relationship with our Lord (John 15; Psalm 119).

Another helpful strategy is to focus on now and live in the moment. Matthew 6:34 says, "Therefore do not worry about tomorrow, for tomorrow will worry about itself. Each day has enough trouble of its own." Yesterday is gone. We can't relive it. Tomorrow isn't here yet. All we truly have is today.

Living one day at a time is hard to do. It's so easy to run ahead. We want to see the end design and understand what God is doing, but the Master's hand often remains hidden. We like order and neatly tied threads, not clashing colors and ugly knots. That's where trust comes in. Trust that He knows what He's doing, has a plan, and is working all things together for good.

When I live in the now and apply these strategies, life's problems are not so overwhelming. The strategies don't remove problems, but they are helpful in finding a path through them.

God used John's counseling, the prayers of many, practical activities, and medication to bring me out of the depression. In the process I discovered that, aside from the cross of Calvary, there's no better setting for God to reveal the extent of His faithful love toward us than when we are in the depths of a painful trial. As I reached the lowest point in my depression, God orchestrated two specific incidents.

The first took place when a neighbor and I were sitting at the dining-room table of a woman and her adult son who wanted to learn more about God. I was turning to a passage in my Bible when I became acutely aware of the fact that they were directing all of their questions to me, not both of us, as had earlier been the case. In that moment, the Lord impressed my mind: *Even though you've written yourself off because of your depression, I haven't written you off. I'm not ashamed of you. I love you! I can use you, I'm still using you, and I'll continue to use you.*

My heart soared with a peace that came with the assurance of God's love for me and the sheer joy of having the privilege of sharing His Word.

The second incident took place soon afterward while on a trip to our hometown of Benton, Pennsylvania. I stopped by the high school to talk to my dad, who was a teacher. As I walked down the hallway, someone said my name. I turned around and saw a teacher. He thanked me for talking to him about the Lord during my senior year. He said he was going through a difficult time in his life and had been reminded of what I had told him. He was thinking about it and wanted me to know that he appreciated my talk with him that day. After a brief exchange, he returned to his classroom and I continued down the hallway.

Immediately the Lord once again impressed upon me the same message. He wasn't ashamed of me. He hadn't written me off. He was still using me. Most of all, He loved me!

That was the turning point in my depression. From then on it was still slow-going, but at least I was heading the right way. God's assurance of His love for me, apart from anything I did or could do, was a liberating force that met me at the bottom and encouraged me that things could get better.

Another lesson I learned is that nothing can get to me without having passed through my heavenly Father's hands first. This is another foundational truth that we can cling to when we go through hard times.

We see it clearly spelled out in the Book of Job when God allowed Satan to afflict Job, but only to the degree that He set as allowable (1:12; 2:6). God is sovereign over everything (Psalm 83:18).

I don't know about you, but that is a tremendous comfort to me.

As only He can do, God brought good out of my experience with depression. If I had not needed John's help, Eric and I would not have learned about our relationship problems. Only the Lord knows what our marriage would be like today if that had not happened.

It's easy to look back at that period of time and clearly see God's faithful hand at work. However, at the time I had no idea what He was doing.

That's how it is when we go through hard times, isn't it? We don't see how God can work it out, let alone use it for good, but we don't have to see it to know it's true. We just have to take Him at His Word.

Romans 8:28 says, "And we know that in all things God works for the good of those who love him, who have been called according to his purpose."

The Master Weaver has a redeeming purpose whenever He chooses to use dark-colored threads in the tapestry of our lives (2 Corinthians 1:3–6).

Chapter 3

Admitting That We Hurt

"GOOD OUT OF bad" sounds like an oxymoron, yet the Creator of the universe specializes in bringing good out of bad. Romans 8 tells us that, with the goal of conforming us into the image of His Son, God works all things together for the good of those who love Him.

There are many facets to the good that God brings out of bad. Our lives are so intertwined, that God's work in one person's life can have repercussions in many other lives. Sometimes we get to see the good that comes out of bad situations; sometimes we won't get to see it this side of eternity. Sometimes it affects only us. Other times God uses what we've gone through for good in someone else's life.

That's what happened to Joseph. His jealous brothers sold him into slavery, and he was taken to Egypt. He was falsely accused and spent many years in jail for a crime he didn't commit. In God's timing, Joseph went directly from a prison cell into Pharaoh's presence and became second in command of Egypt! How's that for a day?

God used the treachery of Joseph's brothers to put him in a position to save countless lives during a famine. He also used it to move Jacob's family to Egypt, where they eventually grew into the Hebrew nation.

After Jacob died, Joseph's brothers feared revenge. They need not have feared. Joseph's deep faith in God had remained intact in spite of what had been done to him.

He told his brothers, "Don't be afraid. Am I in the place of God? You intended to harm me, but God intended it for good to accomplish what is now being done, the saving of many lives" (Genesis 50:19–20).

What a marvelous confession of faith in God's sovereignty, even over painful events!

Have you ever felt sidelined as a Christian because you were going through a hard time? When I was experiencing depression, I felt as if it was holding me back from doing something productive. I didn't think anything good could come out of it.

In Romans 5, Paul speaks of a positive progression of spiritual change that can take place in us as we go through trials. The progression begins with suffering and ends with the love of God being real to us. Although trials are painful, they can be profitable.

The heat of affliction and the painful blows of trials combine to forge valuable traits in us as nothing else can. James 1 tells us that the testing of our faith develops perseverance and gives us a chance to grow in our endurance.

I'm reminded of the butterfly. A butterfly's struggle to get out of its cocoon is part of God's design to strengthen it. Without that struggle, it dies because it isn't able to develop the muscles it needs to fly and to eat. In the same way, God wants to use our trials to develop and strengthen us. Suffering has been a part of life for God's people across the ages, and it plays a vital role in God's plan (1 Peter 4:12; James 5:10). He used another trial to teach me this truth, and I've discovered it to be another foundational building block when facing hard times.

It began in the summer of 1986, when I joined the ladies' softball team at my church. Our first game was my last. While playing shortstop, I dove for a ball and injured my neck and left shoulder.

The series of events that followed changed the course of my life. I'm not the person today that I would have been if I had not been injured. God used what occurred to shape and mold me in positive ways that probably would not have happened if not for the injury. He also used it to equip me and to give me a platform from which to minister to others.

We read in 2 Corinthians 1:3–4: "Praise be to the God and Father of our Lord Jesus Christ, the Father of compassion and the God of all comfort, who comforts us in all our troubles, so that we can comfort those in any trouble with the comfort we ourselves have received from God."

I've seen the truth in this verse work itself out many times over the years as God has used the hard times He's brought me through to enable me to reach out to others. I've been able to identify with people I wouldn't have been able to identify with had it not been for those hard times.

God has given me the privilege of talking with many people, some of whom I have never met in person. Sometimes my friends have asked me to talk with people they know. At times people pour out their pain and break down in tears simply because they are talking with someone who can identify with them.

Whenever God uses what I've been through to help someone else, I am profoundly grateful for His ability to work all things together for good. No, I haven't enjoyed the painful events that have touched my life, but seeing God use them to minister to others makes me marvel at His sovereign plan and thankful for His redeeming purpose in everything I go through.

My softball game injury led to three surgeries, the last of which took place in August 1988.

When I was discharged following the third surgery, I had no idea that a chronic health problem was about to surface. Unknown to my husband and me, while I was in the hospital my immune system succumbed to chronic fatigue syndrome, or CFS as it's called. I became ill with symptoms that came and went without rhyme or reason. We began a frustrating search to discover the cause of my illness.

Long before we received a diagnosis, an unfortunate interaction with far-reaching consequences took place.

Did you know that we leave fingerprints in each other's lives? We can't see them, but they're there. Did you also know there is a right time and a wrong time to say something to a person, especially to one who's going through a hard time?

Proverbs 25:20 compares a person who takes away a garment on a cold day with one who sings songs to a heavy heart. Proverbs 12:18

says, "Reckless words pierce like a sword, but the tongue of the wise brings healing."

One afternoon I received a phone call from a friend that left a lasting fingerprint in my life. She said, "I just called to see how you're doing. So, how are you doing?"

I hesitated a moment, considering how much to say. I knew she cared and was praying, so I decided to tell her exactly how I was doing. I told her how sick I was and that we still didn't know why. I told her I felt like a child because I was so weak that my mom had to bathe me and help me go to the bathroom. Plus, my shoulder was still in a sling with a swath around my chest, and I was in a great deal of pain.

When I finished talking there was a brief silence, and then she said, "Well, just praise the Lord!" The next thing I heard was the click of her hanging up.

Those words put me on an emotional roller coaster that consumed the energy I needed to get well. What they said to me was that all I had to do was praise the Lord and everything would be okay and I wouldn't struggle anymore. I feared that my continuing emotional struggles were disappointing God.

Over the months that followed, I spent countless hours thinking and praying, trying to settle the issue. Every time I came to the conclusion that God understood my struggles and I wasn't letting Him down, I felt relieved. It never lasted long though. From deep within, a persistent thought arose again and again. *What if she's right? If she's right, then I'm letting God down, and I don't want to do that!*

I needed to know the truth, so I searched the Scriptures on a quest to answer the question, *How do we face the trials in life emotionally?*

Depending on the trial, there is a wide variety of feelings that can come. Maybe you can identify with some responses I've had. Pain—physical, mental, emotional; fear; a desire for escape; disbelief that it is really happening; an intense, all-consuming longing for relief; a longing for things to go back to the way they were; a desire for the nightmare to end, so all of life doesn't have to continue to revolve around such a painful circumstance or situation.

Our emotions can be raw. Sometimes it seems as though a thick cloudbank rolled in and our strong tie to God isn't quite as tight as it was a minute ago.

We can be ultrasensitive to what others say. As believers, we often have our "spiritual antennas" up, trying to process everything we hear from God in order to figure out what He's doing or saying. We need to be careful though, because not everything that's said to us will be from God. Just like that phone call I received. That wasn't God speaking to me.

God spoke to me through the actions of our church family at West Side. Many people called and sent cards to encourage me and to assure me of their prayer support. I was warmed by the kind greetings that friends would pass through Eric on Sundays.

One day, a leader in our church named John Molner called to see how I was doing. Awhile later, there was a knock at the door. It was John. After he'd hung up the phone, he decided he wanted to pray with us in person, so he got in his car and drove over to do just that. A few months later, John also surprised Eric by showing up before a surgery I was about to have. He waited with Eric until it was over.

Over the years, I had numerous surgeries. Another West Side leader, Chuck Bassett, faithfully came to pray before the surgeries. I always requested to be "first on deck" on surgery days, but the 6:00 AM arrival times never deterred Chuck.

Friends provided many marvelous meals, often delivered fresh from the oven just in time for dinner.

Carol Cassara took me to doctor appointments and kept an eye on Benjamin during them. She also took over our family's laundry for many months, swapping clean, pressed clothes for dirty in the church parking lot.

Over time, Eric and I became close friends with John Lohman and his wife, Lin. Lin taught at West Side's preschool. Three-and-a-half-year-old Benjamin went with her to the preschool when the students were practicing for their spring Olympics program. Benjamin proved to be a quick study. One day, shortly after Lin brought him home, his voice carried clear and strong from the bathroom, "And now, ladies and gentlemen, Benjamin James Longnecker will attempt to walk all the way around the toilet without falling in!" God knew I could use a little comic relief!

Our friend, Linda Cribbs, stopped by one day with a melt-in-your-mouth oversize muffin. She said she was in the area and thought of me and thought I would enjoy a treat.

Some people came as if they were sent. One time a knock on the door quickly ushered in my friend walking past me and continuing down the hall as she said, "Hi, Maureen. I only have half an hour, but I thought I'd stop by and do some cleaning for you. So, what needs to be cleaned the most? Probably your bathroom, so that's what I'll do."

I could give more examples, but I think you can see that God used His church to show His love to our family. That's one way God spoke to me.

That's also how my weakness became an opportunity for God to show His strength. Trials actually have more to do with God's strength than our weakness. In any trial, God is our strength; however, He doesn't usually act in a vacuum. God's ways of strengthening people center around the body of believers reaching out and ministering His love to those in need. It was a powerful testimony to many people as they watched West Side minister to our family.

Another way God spoke to me was through His Word. I studied the lives of Jesus and Paul and learned from their encounters with suffering.

Jesus' evening in the Garden of Gethsemane was an intensely painful time for Him emotionally, and He wanted companionship (Matthew 26). He took His disciples with Him to the garden. Once there, He took the three He was closest to a little farther. He wanted to talk to the Father, but He wanted friends near Him as well.

We too need to talk to the Father, but we also need friends, because the only thing worse than the pain of a trial is trying to bear it alone.

Jesus began to be sorrowful and troubled.

Have you ever felt that way because of something you were facing? I sure have. There is no sin in this. It simply marks us as human. Don't forget; Jesus was fully God and fully man.

Jesus told His friends how He felt, and He didn't gloss over it. He said He was exceedingly sorrowful and asked them to be a part of what was going on by staying close and watching with Him.

Have you ever wanted to have people nearby when you were going through a hard time? Are you honest with your family and friends when you're facing a trial, or do you make light of matters? There's nothing wrong with being honest with others or with asking them to be near you.

Jesus wanted some time with His Father by Himself. He went about a stone's-throw farther into the garden alone. He asked that, if it was possible, He not have to go through with what He was facing, but He also submitted His will to the Father's.

Jesus acknowledged His Father's power over all things. He asked God to use His power to take away the impending suffering but also acknowledged that He wasn't necessarily going to use His power to deliver Jesus out of the situation.

Have you ever asked God to get you out of a trial? There's nothing wrong with that. However, we need to remember to submit our will to His will, even when we ask Him to remove something from us.

Jesus went back and found His friends asleep. He woke them and repeated His desire to have them watch. He told them to pray also so they wouldn't be tempted. Satan will attempt to use the hard times we go through to try to get between us and God.

Jesus told His friends that the spirit was indeed willing, but the flesh was weak. Sometimes we incorrectly think that just because the flesh is weak, the spirit isn't willing. That isn't always true.

Jesus went away a second time and prayed the same way. Then He checked on His friends again. He left them and went off to pray a third time. Once again, He prayed the same thing.

Did you ever ask God something more than once? Jesus did! When our hearts are heavy, we need to keep talking to the Father, even if we're saying the same thing over and over again.

Jesus kept going back and forth between the Father and His friends. It wasn't one to the exclusion of the other.

Some people believe it's a mark of spiritual maturity not to speak up about painful trials. If you ever feel pressured to keep something to yourself, remember that even Jesus wanted His friends to know exactly how He was feeling, and He wanted them to be present.

Luke tells us that an angel appeared and strengthened Jesus. Can you imagine being strengthened by an angel you could actually see? I would have thought that once the supernatural angel visibly appeared and ministered to Him, Jesus would have gained some observable measure of relief. Not so. In the next verse, Luke, the physician, records, "And being in anguish, he prayed more earnestly, and his sweat was like drops of blood falling to the ground" (Luke 22:44).

Do you realize the significance of that verse? Even His spirit being ministered to by an angel didn't take away the severe emotional response Jesus was experiencing. If you are ever in emotional agony and have physical symptoms because of it, you're in very good company.

Also notice, the greater the agony, the more earnestly He prayed. We need to keep calling out to Him and not allow pain to short-circuit our relationship.

One statement Jesus made on the cross caught my attention in a new way. It's His famous, "My God, my God, why have you forsaken me?" (Matthew 27:46).

I've often heard it said that Christians should never ask God *why*. Jesus asked why, and He was the only person who ever faced a trial and already knew exactly why it was happening! Yet He still asked the question.

I also saw that Jesus experienced deep agony at the feeling of abandonment by His Father. Have you ever felt abandoned and forsaken by God? I have. There have been times when it seemed as though my prayers were going no farther than the ceiling. Sometimes, when Heaven has been silent, it has felt as though my prayers were bouncing off the ceiling and coming back to hit me on the head, mocking me for praying in the first place. Silence is hard.

Jesus understands our feelings of abandonment. We need to continue to call out to the Father as Jesus did.

Hebrews 5:7 records, "During the days of Jesus' life on earth, he offered up prayers and petitions with loud cries and tears to the one who could save him from death, and he was heard because of his reverent submission."

Jesus experienced very strong emotions. Why should we expect anything less?

After studying Jesus' emotional responses, I looked at Paul's life. In 2 Corinthians 1:8, Paul said he wanted the believers to know about the hardships he'd suffered. In spite of his example, many people think they should suffer silently.

Unless we learn to allow ourselves and others to openly express the painful fallout from living in a sin-tainted world, there will always be a great temptation when we face hard times. That temptation is to put on a mask and keep our problems and genuine feelings to ourselves. When we do this, two things happen for sure. First, masks short-circuit God's plan for people to comfort and help one another. Second, masks isolate those who need help, making their pain even greater.

Paul sure didn't have a mask on when he said he despaired even of life because of the trials he went through in Asia (2 Corinthians 1:8). His candid account reveals how he dealt with his emotional upheaval. In the midst of his despair, Paul made the decision to set his hope on God (vv. 9–10). He trusted God to deliver him, and he enlisted people's prayer support.

We need each other, but we can't be there for others if we don't have any clue what's going on in their lives. Romans 12:15 says, "Rejoice with those who rejoice; mourn with those who mourn." How can we do that if we don't know what someone is feeling or what they're going through?

We can't. That happens only when we follow Jesus' and Paul's model of open and honest communication during painful trials.

As I realized that acknowledging my feelings didn't mean I was letting the Lord down, I began to find freedom in my heart.

The Master knows that dark threads bring pain, and He doesn't expect us to act as if they don't.

Chapter 4

Finding the Freedom of Forgiveness

WESTERN CULTURE PLACES excessive value on tough individualism and independence. Needing help is often viewed as a sign of weakness or failure. Nothing could be further from the truth, especially within the Body of Christ.

First Corinthians 12 uses the term "body" to describe the church. It projects an image of various parts working together and stresses the importance of every part, no matter how large or small.

The bottom line is—we need each other.

It's easier to give than it is to receive. Many of us enjoy helping others but are hesitant to accept help.

When I came down with CFS, I didn't have any choice about admitting my need because it was obvious I couldn't function properly. Our church family stepped in to help. Initially, it was an unsettling experience to have so many people helping me on a regular basis. The sheer amount of help given prohibited the possibility of being able to "pay back" the kindnesses.

Over time, I began to accept their help without my pride getting in the way. I thought about how I feel when I'm able to help others and realized my friends experienced that same joy when they helped me. I also realized that my inclination to try to keep score so I could pay them back isn't what being part of the body is all about. There isn't any payback necessary when God uses people to reach out with His love.

Sometimes people don't accept help. One summer, a couple of friends and I tried to help a friend from church who was ill. Three of us went to her house unannounced with our cleaning supplies. We had to leave because she was so embarrassed by the state of her house that she couldn't accept our help.

Whenever I sense myself starting to shy away from accepting help, I revisit that event and allow myself to feel the deep disappointment I felt when robbed of the opportunity to help.

There truly is joy in giving, but we can't always be in the giving position. If we aren't willing to be on the receiving end when we're in need, we prevent others from experiencing the joy of giving. We also effectively short-circuit what God wants to do in the situation. He wants to use others to minister His loving care to us, but how can He do that if we refuse to accept help?

In Philippians 4:10–19, Paul commended the Philippian believers for the help he received from them and said that God viewed their help as fruit that would abound to their account. God considers what we do for others as being an acceptable and well-pleasing sacrifice to Him.

Matthew 10:42 says, "And if anyone gives even a cup of cold water to one of these little ones because he is my disciple, I tell you the truth, he will certainly not lose his reward." It amazes me that God uses us to do good works and then rewards us for it!

When we use the gifts we received from God to serve others, we administer His grace to them (1 Peter 4:8–11).

Galatians 6:10 says, "Therefore, as we have opportunity, let us do good to all people, especially to those who belong to the family of believers." We're to be known for our love for one another (Romans 12:9–10).

Matthew 5:16 says, "In the same way, let your light shine before men, that they may see your good deeds and praise your Father in heaven." God is glorified when believers minister to others in love and good deeds.

God often uses believers as His channel of blessing. Sometimes blessings come at the most amazing times and in the most amazing ways.

Years ago, when we were still in the missionary internship, we had an unexpected blessing one evening. Eric and I had talked about wanting to go out to eat, but we knew we couldn't afford it. At dinnertime, we pulled into our parking lot after running errands. We were surprised to see one of our friends from church, John Westerlund, waiting for us on the front steps of our building. As soon as he saw us, he broke into one of his characteristic smiles. He came over to our car and handed Eric a gift of money through the open window. He said he felt he was supposed to give it to us so we could go out to eat.

We felt incredibly loved—by John and by the Lord! I was deeply moved by the fact that God cared about our desire for something that wasn't necessary. It seemed a lavish use of money. Yet God's instruction for its use was clear in John's message. God wanted us to go out to eat. What a kind and gracious God! Nothing in our life is too small for Him.

One month our rent was due soon, and we were nowhere close to being able to pay it. We prayed, but days passed without a solution. On the final day, as soon as the mailman left our building, I raced downstairs for our mail. Eric and I quickly scanned through the return addresses. The only personal letter we had received was from a college student. We were both disappointed. College students are notorious for needing money, not giving it. I opened the envelope to read the letter and found a check for the exact amount we needed for our rent payment. He'd proven Himself faithful once again!

One of the ways God shows His love is in the personally tailored lessons He teaches us. I can see how God was weaving His threads into the tapestry of my life even before I began a personal relationship with Him. He was looking out for me, designing events to build my character, and equipping me with traits that I would need later on. He knew what I would face in life, and He knew I needed to understand that He's trustworthy. He orchestrated countless details and circumstances, steadily increasing my trust in Him.

When I think of my life before I accepted Jesus as my Savior, I'm reminded of Paul's description of the unsaved Israelites. He said they were zealous for God, but their zeal wasn't based on knowledge. They didn't know the righteousness that comes from God, so they tried to establish their own. In so doing, they didn't submit to God's righteousness (Romans 10:1–4). That describes my life until I was twelve years old.

I grew up in a very close-knit family with my parents and younger brother, Jimmy. We were religious and loved God, but we didn't understand what it means to have a personal relationship with Jesus Christ. We were faithful to our church and sincere in our adherence to its teachings.

My entire extended family lived within a forty-five-minute drive of our house. I felt very secure growing up surrounded by people who cared about me.

In spite of the love and sense of belonging I experienced, I had an underlying nagging sense that something was missing. Unknown to me, the unsettling feeling was reflective of the void in my life because of my sinful condition that separated me from God (Romans 3:23; 6:23).

I was very aware that I sinned on a regular basis, and I felt the weight of my guilt. I wanted to know for sure that I was forgiven by God, but I didn't see how I could know that. Whatever feelings of forgiveness I did experience never lasted long.

In April 1976, my best friend, Sharon Longnecker, invited me to a special meeting at her church. That evening the guest speaker presented the simple plan of salvation. For the first time, I heard the whole story. I'd always believed that Jesus was the Son of God (Mark 1:10–11), that He died on the cross for my sins (Romans 5:6–11), and that He was buried and rose again the third day (Mark 15:43–47; 16:1–14).

I didn't know that salvation is a free gift that needs to be received. Intellectual knowledge about Christ isn't enough (James 2:19). To have our sins forgiven requires action on our part, not just mental assent. We need to confess our sinful condition, repent of our sins, and ask God to forgive us (Romans 10:10, 13; Acts 4:12). We need to accept the gift of forgiveness (Ephesians 2:8–9). I had been trying to earn God's favor by doing good works, but good works can't cover sin or take away its penalty (Galatians 2:16; Titus 3:5; 2 Timothy 1:9). I had to come to God on His terms, not the way I assumed was acceptable to Him (Proverbs 16:25; Romans 10:1–4).

When Jesus died on the cross, He took upon Himself the punishment we deserved for our sin (2 Corinthians 5:19–21). He paid our death penalty. Now, God the Father offers us a legal pardon for our sins because of Jesus' shed blood on the cross (Romans 5:1–11; Hebrews 9:11–28). Religion is man's way of trying to reach God, but salvation is God's provision for Him to reach man (Romans 3:19–20; John 1:10–13; 1 Timothy 2:3–6). I hadn't known I needed to pray and ask Jesus to forgive my sins and receive His gift of salvation (John 3:16–18).

I felt as though a light bulb turned on, and blinders fell off. That's what was missing! At the end of the service, with the pastor's wife present, I prayed and received God's gift of salvation. As I prayed, the long-desired elusive feeling of forgiveness flooded my heart. The void vanished. I had been forgiven by the only One who had the authority to forgive me (Luke 5:18–26).

When I walked out the door of the building, I felt as though physical weights had been lifted from my shoulders. I felt lighter. The heavy weight of guilt was gone, and I reveled in the freedom of forgiveness.

That evening was the beginning of a new life for me and eventually for my entire family. Mom recommitted her life to Christ that same evening, having received Him as her Savior in her childhood. She had not grown much spiritually in the intervening years; however, after that night, she began to grow quickly. My brother made a profession of faith in Christ soon after I did. Four years later, Dad also placed his faith in Christ.

Chapter 5

Learning to Trust

AS A NEW Christian, I had much to learn. Peter states, "Like newborn babies, crave pure spiritual milk, so that by it you may grow up in your salvation, now that you have tasted that the Lord is good" (1 Peter 2:2–3). God faithfully provided positive spiritual influences in my life and placed me in a wonderful environment to help me grow spiritually.

My friendship with Sharon deepened, and I took my first baby steps as a Christian with her assistance. I learned a lot by observing how she lived and how her relationship with the Lord made a difference in her life. I enjoyed reading my Bible and attending church services. Youth-group meetings and Sunday-school classes provided excellent teaching that began to ground me in biblical truths.

Pastor Longnecker was a gifted expository preacher. The rippling of pages was a familiar sound during his sermons as we flipped through our Bibles and compared Scripture with Scripture.

The people who attended the church were warm and friendly, and I formed many close bonds. Each Sunday and Wednesday night, Pastor Longnecker allowed people to share prayer requests and tell what God was doing in their lives. Their testimonies taught me that God is powerful and that He's active in people's lives. Regularly meeting with other believers caused me to grow in my faith (Hebrews 10:24–25).

My home life was an important part in my overall development as well. The immense amount of time spent together as a family was a precious gift my parents gave me. I talked everything over with my parents and with my mom in particular. She and I shared many late nights as I talked over life's events and benefited from her advice.

My mom spent time each day in prayer and Bible study and listened to a Christian radio station. Her growing understanding of God's Word and her deepening relationship with the Lord made an impact on me and strengthened my own walk with Him.

The summer after my junior year of high school, I went through an intensive, three-week leadership training course at a Christian camp. The program emphasized developing a personal relationship with Christ and taught us how to share our faith.

Each day was full of learning and responsibilities. I saw God work in powerful ways. He brought our group safely through a backpacking trip along the Appalachian Trail. We encountered a rattlesnake, weathered a severe storm, and saw Him provide water when the source our leaders counted on was dried up. When the program ended, I accepted the camp's offer of a job as a junior counselor for the rest of the summer.

While I was growing spiritually at camp, my dad was on his own spiritual journey at home. As he studied the Word of God, he found many contradictions between what the Scriptures said and what he had always believed. One day Dad talked to a friend of his about it while they were fishing. Dad's friend encouraged him to believe what the Bible says and to accept it as the authority rather than to hold to what people have said is true. Dad realized he needed to reject man's opinions when they conflict with God's Word. As soon as Dad got home from fishing, he went to his bedroom and prayed to accept the Lord. The following weekend, he and Mom visited me at camp to tell me the good news. I was thrilled!

I had the opportunity to see God at work changing the lives of some of our campers. One camper, whose nickname was Peaches, instigated more fights than all the others combined. He was strong and aggressive. A natural leader, he gathered other boys around him, only to target weaker boys.

The counselors who were assigned to Peaches voiced concern about letting him finish out the week. At a staff meeting one morning, the leaders debated whether or not to allow Peaches to stay. At the end, we decided to let him stay and prayed for his salvation and for the safety of everyone involved.

Peaches continued to be sullen and unresponsive to the staff, and he continued to cause fights. Nothing broke through his hard shell. When the last day of camp arrived, the staff breathed a collective sigh of relief that Peaches would soon be on his way home. We were soon to be surprised. When the camp gathered for a final campfire, Peaches announced he had accepted Christ as Savior!

The experiences that summer impacted me in many ways, maturing my faith and forging in my heart an even greater desire to be involved in full-time ministry.

One of the biggest lessons I began to learn that summer had to do with God working all things together for good, as His Word says in Romans 8:28: "And we know that in all things God works for the good of those who love him, who have been called according to his purpose."

My first encounter with that verse took place before I was a believer. At the time, my parents were involved in a Bible study and my dad printed it on a three-by-five card in black marker to memorize it.

Then the Lord brought it to my attention at camp. That fall, during my senior year of high school, God again impressed my mind with Romans 8:28. By that time I was dating Sharon's older brother, Eric. The two of us talked about its meaning.

We realized it isn't hard to believe that God works all things together for good during the easy times. What about the rough times? Does it apply then? What exactly does "all things" mean?

I didn't know that my interest in the verse was going to accompany me into my adulthood or that it would become my favorite verse. When God called my attention to it early in my relationship with Him, He began weaving a brightly colored thread into the tapestry of my life. It was a thread He knew would play a vital role later on.

In the fall of 1981, I entered Washington Bible College to continue preparing to be a missionary. God used my years there to further drive home the fact of His faithfulness and trustworthiness and to continue to deepen my relationship with Him.

My favorite Christian service team was the evangelism team that went to the Mall in Washington, DC, to witness. Through this ministry, I grew in my prayer life and in my understanding of the Holy Spirit's work in people's lives. I began to rely on Him to answer prayer specifically and to give direction on whom to talk to and when. Between our weekend trips, I prayed for Him to prepare people's hearts for the gospel and for Him to lead me to them the following Sunday.

One week I prayed for two people to accept Christ. I also prayed that God would cause them to feel empty inside and to know that there must be more to life than what they were experiencing. All week I prayed the same way. On Sunday, I went into one of the museums and asked the Lord for direction. I noticed an empty bench on the right side of the foyer and sat down. Not long after I sat down, someone joined me. I asked the Lord if it was the person I was to talk to, but didn't feel He was giving a positive answer. I continued to pray. Numerous people came and went. I began to wonder if I would run out of time before I talked to anyone. A man sat down and I glanced over at him. Even though I didn't have any indication from the Lord that I should speak yet, I was tempted to speak to him anyhow.

As soon as I determined to wait for the Lord's leading instead of venturing out on my own, the man stood up and left. Immediately, two women joined me on the bench. This time there was a positive leading from Him, and I quickly prayed for His guidance.

The two ladies of Spanish descent were a mother and her adult daughter. The mother spoke only Spanish, and the daughter spoke both Spanish and English. In a mixture of both languages, we began to learn about each other, and I shared the gospel with them. The daughter translated for her mother.

They listened attentively and tears pooled in their eyes. They told me they had been feeling empty inside. In fact, just that morning when they were participating in their church's service, they had felt that something was missing and that there had to be more to life than what they were experiencing.

I shouldn't have been surprised, but I was. It was incredible to hear exactly what I had prayed for God to put in someone's heart come out of their mouths so clearly. They bowed their heads and prayed out loud, asking Jesus to forgive them and come into their lives. Then they started exclaiming about things they now understood. Words to hymns they had always sung held new meaning. They sang a couple of songs and then asked me questions until I had to leave.

I marveled at what God had done. It was humbling and amazing to see God work so specifically in answer to prayer!

When I thought of my temptation to speak to someone without the Lord's leading, I was thankful God had kept me from trying to witness in my own strength. Only the Spirit of God, using the Word of God, does the work of God in a person's life. I was thankful He had kept me from getting in His way.

It became obvious that Satan didn't like my growing relationship with the Lord or the witnessing I was doing with the team. He attacked me with an intensity that shook me to the core. I had nightmares so terrifying that I awakened drenched in sweat. In my dreams, I felt as though I was fighting a spiritual force that was trying to pull my spirit from my body. It happened every night. I dreaded going to sleep and became afraid to continue advancing on Satan's turf.

Eric and I prayed together for deliverance from the nightly occurrence, but it continued. One evening, the head of our evangelism team and another good friend joined us to pray. From that night on, the dreams left.

I learned many lessons from that experience, and I was able to see how God worked all things together for good. I learned that Satan is a formidable foe who seeks to stop those who want to tell others about Christ. I also saw the power of praying together as a small group. I learned a healthy respect for Satan's power, but I also learned that the Holy Spirit inside me is greater than Satan (1 John 4:4).

The alertness to watch for ways in which God worked all things together for good became an even greater focus for me. I had many opportunities to put it into practice that year.

During a freshman orientation soccer game, I aggravated my lower back where I had injured it playing basketball in high school.

God used this setback for good. I had been assigned to work in the kitchen to earn money toward my tuition. Washing tables after meals made my back ache, so they offered me the job of evening receptionist for the college.

I was thrilled with the new job! One of the benefits was the freedom to do school work during slow times. I didn't know of any other job on campus like that. I marveled at what God had done for me.

One day the supply of quarters I had brought with me for the laundry machines ran out. I asked God to provide money for me to wash my clothes. After praying, I changed into shorts, as it was hot. I chose a pair I hadn't yet worn at college. As I pulled them up, I felt something bulky in the right pocket. Curious as to what I had left in there, I slid my hand inside and pulled out a plastic sandwich bag full of quarters! I stared at the money and tried, without success, to recall putting it in my pocket. Although I didn't understand how He'd done it, I knew God had answered my prayers.

It was as though He kept extending His hand toward me and beckoning me to trust Him. Each small instance of seeing His hand working on my behalf laid another foundational stone in what was becoming a deeper faith and a willingness to trust Him with harder situations. I was yet to learn just how hard.

Chapter 6

Guarding Our Hearts

HAVE YOU EVER fallen into the trap of thinking you're able to handle anything and everything on your own? Have you ever thought you're smart enough, strong enough, or just plain stubborn enough to solve any problem? I have.

Christmas break during my freshman year of college was the first time I was confronted with my erroneous thinking in this area. It was unsettling to discover I'm not as self-reliant as I thought I was, but the experience enabled me to find out that God is who He says He is!

The atmosphere when I arrived home for Christmas break shocked me. A heavy gloom permeated every room. One would never have guessed it was so close to Christmas. The complete absence of decorations was strange and ominous by itself. As I tried to find out what was going on, the story came out.

My dad was in a deep depression, unknown to everyone except Mom. For years he had struggled with a poor self-image, but he portrayed an outwardly confident bearing. The man who was the life of the party and always looked out for others lived in an internal dark world of depression.

Seventeen years passed before I did some reading and learned that Dad matched the profile for bipolar disorder. After talking with health-care professionals about it, I believe that was Dad's problem. However, that Christmas, there was no knowledge of it.

In fact, Dad's longstanding underlying depression wasn't even the focus. The fallout from a verbal blow directed at Mom took center stage. One day while I had been at college, Dad let loose with a tirade, reciting a long list of things Mom had done in the past. It was as though he had never forgiven or forgotten anything she had ever done wrong, even though she had apologized and they were supposedly resolved long before. Mom emotionally reeled and then plummeted in the aftermath. By the time I arrived for Christmas, she was in a severe depression.

My parents and brother were three hurting people who didn't know what to do. Each of them was willing to do things with me, and did so. However, they seemed unable to do things with each other as we had always done. I pulled out the Christmas decorations and put them up in an attempt to get my family out of the doldrums. I poured myself into trying to correct a situation that was far beyond my understanding, abilities, and control.

As the time to return to college approached, I wrestled with the question of whether or not I should drop out. I wasn't accustomed to walking away from an unfinished job, and I felt responsible to correct the problems and get my family back to normal. Since that hadn't occurred yet, I wondered what I should do.

Eric's mom advised me to return to college and trust God to use someone else in my family's lives. Even though I'd learned a lot about trusting God, it was a hard decision. I couldn't imagine who He could—or would—use to replace me. Although I didn't know what to do in the situation, at least I could be there and try to find answers. I didn't know of anyone who played a large enough role in their lives to understand what was going on and would be able to devote the time and energy necessary to help.

I began to realize that part of trusting God is not knowing what He will do, yet counting on Him to work out the details. So, with a heavy heart and an exhausted body, I returned to school. I walked into my dorm room, laid down on my bed without removing my coat, and woke up fourteen hours later.

Even though I had returned because I believed that God would take care of my family, it was hard to concentrate on my studies. My mind continually wandered back to Benton, and I wondered what was happening. I kept thinking about Romans 8:28 and wondering what God was going to do. Trusting God with that situation was the biggest test of my faith I had ever faced.

As part of my preparation for missionary service, I applied to go to Peru for a summer missionary program. I wanted to get some experience living and serving in the country I anticipated moving to someday. Eric had already spent two summers in Peru and one in Bolivia.

Raising the funds I needed provided another opportunity to watch God work on my behalf. Family and friends were very generous in their support of me, and the money was provided in plenty of time. Later, as my faith deepened and my experience in trusting the Lord grew, His provision wouldn't always come so early, but it always arrived on time.

I thoroughly enjoyed my summer in Peru. Our team worked with missionaries who lived in Iquitos, a large city in the Amazon jungle. We also traveled by houseboat on the Amazon River and visited several villages along the way to an evangelistic conference in the town of Nauta.

The day we returned from Nauta, I took a nap and woke up extremely dizzy. The missionaries rushed me to the doctor, and I spent the remaining time in Peru mostly in bed. Fortunately it happened at the end of the summer.

Nobody understood what caused my dizziness. Years later we discovered that it was because of my allergy to mold.

The missionaries did a wonderful job of acquainting us with as many types of ministry as possible. It was a privilege to get to know them and to serve with them for a short time. The experience made me eager to finish my education and go back as a career missionary.

The day I returned from Peru, Eric asked me to marry him. Ten months later, in the early summer of 1984, we were married. We were brimming with ideas and plans for what we anticipated would be a life of serving God together as missionaries in Peru.

Everything we had done individually to that point had been done with that goal in mind, and we began our marriage eager to face the remaining prerequisites together. We had no idea that our future would be so different than we anticipated.

Right from the beginning of our marriage, God showed His faithfulness to us.

After our honeymoon, Eric and I worked for a cleaning company. A month and a day after our wedding, I had emergency surgery to remove my appendix, and that ended my working career. By the time I was recovered from the operation, I was sick with morning sickness from my first pregnancy. Then school began for my final year.

We soon realized that Eric wasn't going to earn as much money as had been indicated by the owner of the company. We prayed about him quitting and searched the newspaper in vain for another job.

Finally, convinced it was the right thing to do, even though he didn't have any prospects for another job, Eric gave his two-week notice. His employer tried to talk him out of it, saying there wasn't any way Eric would find another job. Eric was shaken up, but he stuck with what he believed the Lord had told him to do.

God brought a job opening to our attention through an ad I saw posted on a bulletin board at the college. Eric applied and was hired. The job not only paid a much higher hourly wage, but it also provided benefits we didn't have. The cleaning company owner was shocked when he heard that Eric would begin working for another company the day after his two-week notice was up.

How we praised God for His gracious provision!

After Eric started his new job, we learned a valuable lesson about applying a scriptural principle in dealing with difficult people. An employee took a dislike to Eric and often harassed him. Eric put up with obnoxious behavior almost daily.

As we prayed about the situation together, the Lord reminded us of a passage in Romans that says not to repay anyone for evil and to overcome evil with good (12:17–21).

One day Eric heard that the guy's girlfriend had delivered a baby, so he bought a baby card and placed it under the windshield wiper of his car. He never mistreated Eric again.

God continued to teach us valuable lessons. He taught us to guard our hearts. Proverbs 4:23 says, "Above all else, guard your heart, for it is the wellspring of life." Our education, Bible study, verse memorization, preparation, and earnest desire to serve the Lord wouldn't mean a thing if we didn't guard our hearts.

Paul said in 1 Corinthians 8:1, "Knowledge puffs up, but love builds up." Knowledge of the Word doesn't guarantee obedience to it. Desire to serve God doesn't guarantee faithfulness to Him.

In Galatians 6:1, Paul says, "Brothers, if someone is caught in a sin, you who are spiritual should restore him gently. But watch yourself, or you also may be tempted."

In other words, we should never consider ourselves beyond temptation. Beginning our walk with the Lord well isn't a guarantee that we will stay faithful to Him.

The Lord used an experience I had while visiting the county jail to teach me this lesson. A friend and I went to witness to the women inmates weekly through the Good News Jail and Prison Ministry. We walked along the catwalk around the perimeter of the women's cell block and initiated conversation through the bars. There was normally a glaring lack of exposure to biblical teaching, even concerning basic topics. I suppose that's why I was astounded by a conversation one day.

I was looking for someone to speak with when an attractive young woman caught my eye and returned my gaze. She was open to talking with me, and soon I was spellbound by her story.

She grew up in a loving Christian home, accepted Christ as her Savior as a child, and attended Christian schools all her life. She had read the entire Bible through several times and had memorized many verses, including some entire books. At one time, she could flip with ease throughout the Bible to answer questions about it.

My mind began to reel as I tried to reconcile what I was hearing with the setting. I looked at her incredulously and blurted out, "Then how in the world did you end up in here?" Chagrined at my impetuousness, I was going to apologize. Instead of taking offense, the woman calmly proceeded to utter words I don't think I'll ever forget. She looked me directly in the eyes and said, "I walked away from the Lord so slowly that I didn't even realize it was happening."

I've replayed that scene in my mind many times since then. Both of us were believers in Christ, but only one of us was free to walk away from the jail that day. The previous depth of her relationship with Christ had not been a guarantee of continuing to follow Him closely.

My mom used to say: "It can happen to the best of us." She was right. Any of us is capable of committing absolutely any sin. Our pride doesn't like to admit the truth of that statement. We would rather think of ourselves as being "above" certain behaviors. A close look at the Scriptures reveals a wide assortment of sins committed by those who were followers of God. As someone has well said, "There, but for the grace of God, go I." We continually need to cultivate a growing relationship with the Lord and not just coast on past experience with Him.

Just as you can't judge a book by its cover, you also can't judge a person by what can be seen on the outside. Jesus made it very clear that it isn't what's on the outside of a person that matters; rather, it's what's on the inside that counts (Matthew 15:17–20). First Samuel 16:7 says, "The LORD does not look at the things man looks at. Man looks at the outward appearance, but the LORD looks at the heart." We get so caught up with the externals that we forget that the heart of a person is what really matters.

Jesus had some very strong words for the hypocritical religious leaders who gave a pretense of righteous living so others would admire them. He compared them to whitewashed tombs, beautiful-looking on the outside, but unclean on the inside (Matthew 23:27–28).

I'm reminded of what happened to a mountain ash tree that was outside our bedroom window. Its leaves were full and its branches were laden with bunches of bright red berries. It looked healthy, productive, and growing. One morning I opened the blinds and discovered the tree had fallen over in the night. It had simply snapped off at ground level because it was rotted out. There'd been no warning signs of the destructive force at work. However, just because it took place unseen didn't mean it wasn't happening. The internal erosion continued until the tree could no longer be supported, and it toppled over.

Too often the Christian community has been shaken by the fall of a prominent Christian leader. Shocked, we ask ourselves, "How could this happen?" Unbelievers sometimes use those occasions to point a mocking finger at Christianity as a whole, thinking they're justified in dismissing it.

There have been many studies on factors contributing to leaders' failures. One recurring theme is the lack of accountability. Isolation in ministry increases vulnerability.

The men's ministry, Promise Keepers, stresses the value of accountability partnerships. My husband is blessed to have a best friend who is also his accountability partner. Their friendship began during the early days of our internship at West Side. After attending a Promise Keepers' event, they took it a step further by writing an accountability agreement. They signed it and have held each other accountable ever since.

I'm so thankful for the role Jeff Wood plays in Eric's life! They're like brothers; they can call on one another anytime for anything. They're open and honest about what's going on in their lives. They pray for each other and check up on one another.

Another aspect of their accountability relationship gives me permission to talk to Jeff anytime I think Eric could use a phone call for any reason. Jeff's wife, Lisa, has the same permission to call Eric about her husband. It's a privilege Lisa and I have both used, and we don't take it for granted. We're both thankful that our husbands are willing to be accountable!

Sometimes the strength of a temptation is diminished simply by telling someone else about it. Satan often changes tactics when we bring another person into the picture, because we aren't as apt to dabble with temptation when we know someone will be checking up on us.

Perhaps if the woman in the jail that day had connected with an accountability partner, it would have changed her path. Instead of being incarcerated, maybe she would have been the one witnessing to the inmates.

After I had been going to the jail for a while, I started having nightmares. I can get claustrophobic, and that was the angle Satan used.

In my dreams, I could hear jail doors slamming behind me as I passed through different security levels in the corridors. As each metallic clang rang out, I was reminded that there was no quick way out of there. I began to wake up damp with sweat and with my heart pounding in fear. I knew it was spiritual warfare, and the stakes were high.

One night I said, "Satan, I know you are just trying to scare me out of going to the jail. Right now, I'm turning the tables on you. The more you make me have these bad nightmares, the more I'll know you don't like what I'm doing and are trying to make me stop. From now on, the harder you try to keep me from going into the jail, the more determined I will be to go. You wouldn't do this if you didn't think it was valuable, so you're going to make me more determined to go, because I recognize the eternal value of what is taking place." The nightmares ended.

Chapter 7

Choosing to Trust

IN OUR MODERN, scientific, technologically-savvy country, it's easy to downplay satanic power. We tend to view everything from the physical realm without realizing there are spiritual forces at work all around us. When we minimize what Satan can do, our indifference gives him the ability to work more effectively. We need to acknowledge the reality of spiritual warfare and learn how to fight back instead of ignoring it and playing into Satan's hands.

We have an enemy. He doesn't wear a red suit and carry a pitchfork, but he likes to be thought of that way. After all, a benign cartoon figure doesn't need to be taken seriously.

The Bible teaches that Satan is an aggressive, formidable enemy. Ephesians 6:10–18 tells us to put on the full armor of God so we can stand against the devil's schemes. First Peter 5:8 says, "Be self-controlled and alert. Your enemy the devil prowls around like a roaring lion looking for someone to devour." That doesn't sound like a harmless cartoon character!

In Isaiah 14:12–14 and Ezekiel 28:11–17, we read about Satan's fall from heaven. Ever since then, he's been trying to get people to believe his lies in order to undermine God.

Genesis 3 records Satan's interaction with Adam and Eve, and the consequent entrance of sin into the human race (Romans 5:12–21). Satan presented himself in a way that didn't alarm them. We need to watch out for Satan's disguises as he attacks. Second Corinthians 11:14–15 tells us that Satan masquerades as an angel of light, and his servants masquerade as servants of righteousness. If we always saw him for who he really is, we would probably walk away from more temptations than we do. The problem is that he makes it look so harmless, enjoyable, and irresistible.

Things aren't always the way they look, are they? When I was a child, I noticed the accumulated frost on the inside of a chest freezer one day. It glistened temptingly, so I tried to take a lick and discovered it wasn't the soft, fluffy treat I anticipated. Looks can definitely be deceiving!

We need to use God's Word to evaluate everything. If something doesn't measure up to that standard, it isn't good, no matter how tempting it may look.

Sin presents itself as a desirable option, but it's an alluring lie. Just like Adam and Eve found out, once the temptation is acted upon, the true nature of sin is revealed.

I've heard a saying that captures this truth. It says, "Sin takes you farther than you want to go, costs you more than you want to pay, and keeps you longer than you want to stay."

When we believe Satan's lies, we're kept in bondage. God wants us to exchange Satan's lies for His truth. Satan twists God's ways for his ungodly purposes.

Romans 1:18–23 tells us that God's creation displays His eternal power and divine nature, but man exchanged the glory of the immortal God for images. Instead of enjoying the beauty and majesty of creation and being drawn to worship the Creator, "They exchanged the truth of God for a lie, and worshiped and served created things rather than the Creator . . ." (1:25).

It began in the Garden of Eden when Satan asked Eve if God had told them not to eat of every tree in the garden. Do you think he asked the question because he wanted clarification on what had been said? No, he wanted to put his own spin on it and plant a seed of doubt in Eve's mind about the character of God.

He pointed out that God had withheld something from Adam and Eve, only he made it look as if God's reason for doing it was arbitrary or unkind. He wanted them to think God was withholding something good from them. In so doing, he wanted them to doubt God's goodness.

Satan wants us to doubt God's character and His love for us. He's still in the business of planting seeds of doubt in people's minds and hearts.

Eve told the serpent that God had said they couldn't eat or touch the fruit of the tree in the middle of the garden, lest they die. That wasn't exactly true. God had told Adam not to eat the fruit from the tree, but the Bible doesn't tell us that He said not to touch it.

We're on dangerous ground when we don't understand God's Word accurately. Manmade additions to God's Word may be said with good intentions, such as to ensure obedience to what God has said, but they're still manmade and should be acknowledged as such.

We should stick with the pure Word of God. God said His Word is powerful and will accomplish His purposes for it (Isaiah 55:11). We need to fill our hearts and minds with Scripture so that we know the truth and can recognize the lies Satan puts before us.

God's Word is where the power is. The farther we get away from it, the weaker we become in the face of Satan's attacks.

In the Gospel of Matthew, Jesus was tempted by Satan three times. Each time, Jesus responded to the temptation with God's Word. He replied, "It is written . . ." (4:4, 7, 10). It's interesting to note that Satan attempted to use the Word inappropriately by quoting from it to tempt Jesus (4:6). Sometimes Satan tries to misuse the Word of God in our lives as well. When Satan tempts us, we need to follow our Savior's example and respond with the Word of God.

We must know God's Word well so we won't be misled or deceived. Psalm 119 speaks of the relationship between knowing God's Word and being steered away from evil.

Second Timothy 2:15 reminds us of the importance of rightly using God's Word: "Do your best to present yourself to God as one approved, a workman who does not need to be ashamed and who correctly handles the word of truth."

In Acts 17, the people of Berea are commended for their habit of examining what they heard to see if it was true by comparing it with the Scriptures.

Satan deals in lies. God deals in truth. We need to guard against Satan's lies and saturate ourselves with the truth of God's Word.

John 8:44 reveals Satan's character: "You belong to your father, the devil, and you want to carry out your father's desire. He was a murderer from the beginning, not holding to the truth, for there is no truth in him. When he lies, he speaks his native language, for he is a liar and the father of lies."

Satan is a liar. Don't expect truth from him. He is on a time-limited quest to keep people from accepting Jesus as their personal Savior and to try to drive wedges between believers and God.

One of the lies Satan uses is, "When God doesn't prevent something bad from happening, it's because He doesn't care." We can equate inactivity with not caring and think, *God must not care about me, or else He wouldn't have let this happen.* We can start to question God—His very existence, His motives, and His character.

In Matthew 27:42, people witnessing the crucifixion said, "'He saved others' they said, 'but he can't save himself! He's the king of Israel! Let him come down now from the cross, and we will believe in him.'" They had seen Jesus in action and knew He had done miracles. Yet, when He refused to act on His own behalf to save Himself from the pain of being crucified, they put their opinion of Him up for review. They didn't understand what He was accomplishing, so they decided what they thought He should do. Then they based their opinion of Him on whether or not He did what they thought. They said if He came off the cross, they would believe Him. If He didn't, they would not.

We run the risk of doing the same thing with Him today when we want Him to act in certain ways—to deliver us or others we love from suffering. If He doesn't, we question what He's doing. Jesus knew what He was doing by staying on the cross. His seeming inactivity was for their good.

As you face trials, don't put your opinion of God up for review. Instead, as a man named Joe Bayly once said, "Don't forget in the darkness what you have learned in the light."

In the heat of the trial, when you are hurting, confused, and life feels totally out of control, don't give up on God. Keep placing your confidence in Him, no matter what comes your way, and no matter how it makes you feel.

God is always close by us, even when we don't feel His presence (Jeremiah 23:23–24). Trials can make it feel as if God isn't even there, or if He is there, He doesn't care. The truth is, He is there, and He cares very deeply.

Sometimes trials cloud our vision similar to the way storm clouds block our view of the stars. On overcast nights, we know the stars are still there, even though we can't see them. In the same way, we can be assured that God is there and is actively at work in situations, even when we don't see Him.

Psalm 143 records a time when David was overwhelmed and struggling. He couldn't see God's hand in his situation, and his emotions were a mess. But he didn't give up on God. Instead, he poured out his heart in an honest plea for help. He recalled the works that God had done for him in the past, and he put his trust in the faithfulness of God to rescue him again. He banked everything on the unfailing love of God.

When we're confronted with situations that are frightening, painful, and unsettling, we have a choice to make. We can either do what David did and cling to the truth found in God's Word about who God is and depend on Him to act in keeping with His unchanging character, or we can believe the lies Satan puts before us and allow the circumstances to change our opinion of God.

Many times we have to wait for His answer. As a person with a Type A personality, I often find it difficult to wait, especially if I'm trying to be patient about it as well!

Psalm 27:14 says, "Wait for the LORD; be strong and take heart and wait for the LORD." Tie the word "wait" with the word "trial" and you have a recipe for an environment ripe with opportunities for growth. Waiting is one of the hardest things we're told to do, but we can wait expectantly because God's faithful character is reliable. He will never leave us or forsake us, and He will accomplish what He promised.

It takes faith to keep choosing to trust God when life hurts. We need patience to allow Him to work out His plan, even when we aren't seeing things unfold as we want them to.

Sometimes we're tempted to take matters into our own hands instead of allowing God to accomplish His plan using His methods in

His timetable. We court disaster when we step in and try to bring about our own ideas using our methods and strength.

Just ask Abraham and Sarah. They can tell you all about what happens when we get ahead of God. In the daily conflict between Jews and Arabs, the entire world sees the result of their "brainstorm" to help God out.

In Genesis 15, God promised that Abraham would have a child. Abraham (Abram at the time) and his wife Sarah (Sarai at the time) were both getting up in years.

Nevertheless, when God told Abraham he would have a son, Abraham responded in faith. He was off to a good start. Then came that little word "wait." That's the part that often causes us to stumble.

Many years later, they were still waiting, so Sarah decided to help God out and speed up the process. Instead of waiting for God to accomplish His will in accordance with His promise, she thought she needed to assist Him and figure out how to make it happen.

She suggested Abraham have a child with her servant, Hagar. "So she said to Abram, 'The LORD has kept me from having children. Go, sleep with my maidservant; perhaps I can build a family through her'" (Genesis 16:2).

It's bad enough that she thought of this alternative plan, but what was worse was the fact that Abraham bought into it! What happened between, "Abram believed the LORD" (Genesis 15:6), and "Abram agreed to what Sarai said" (Genesis 16:2)? A lot of waiting is what happened.

When God didn't come through with His promise on their timetable, they decided they needed a different strategy. Instead of continuing to look to God to fulfill His promise, they looked around them at the culture in which they lived. In that day, childless women were often shamed by others. This led to the custom of a barren woman giving her servant to her husband in order to produce an heir. Babies born to the servant were considered to be the children of the wife, even though they weren't her biological children.

Abraham and Sarah's decision to use Hagar to bear a child fit with the cultural custom of the day. However, it reflected their lack of trust in God.

Sarah's declaration that God had kept her from having children put the focus on the wrong thing. Instead of waiting for God to keep His promise, they relied on their own wisdom and understanding. Abraham took Sarah's advice, and Ishmael was born by Hagar. Abraham was eighty-six years old when Ishmael was born.

Thirteen years later, the Lord appeared to Abraham again and told him Sarah would have a son (Genesis 17:1–22). Instead of accepting God's Word as truth, Abraham questioned it, and tried to convince God that Ishmael could be the one to live under God's promised blessing.

God told Abraham that Sarah would give birth to a son named Isaac and that He would establish an everlasting covenant with Isaac for his descendants after him (Genesis 17:19). Isaac—the child born of the promise, not Ishmael, the child born of Sarah's servant—would be the one to receive the blessing God had promised would come through Abraham. God was going to work out His plan, in spite of Abraham and Sarah's unnecessary intervention.

God kept His promise to Abraham, and He keeps His promises to us. When things look like they aren't turning out the way we want them to, we have to remember that God is working out His plan, no matter what it looks like to us. He sees the other side of the tapestry. He knows what He's doing. We need to be patient and wait for God to use His methods and not take matters into our own hands.

Chapter 8

Keeping Our Eyes on Him

IN MATTHEW 14, the Lord sent the disciples into a storm. They came out of it with a better understanding of the God who controls circumstances. Their faith in Him was strengthened because of the experience. That's exactly what God wants to accomplish in our lives as we face the trials He allows to come our way. We seem to have a much higher learning curve when we're in situations that are obviously out of our control.

Just before this, Jesus performed the miracle of the feeding of five thousand men with five loaves and two fish. There were twelve baskets of leftovers. That isn't exactly an everyday occurrence. You'd think the disciples would have gotten a good idea of who Jesus is from that miracle. Apparently they didn't.

After that, Jesus made the disciples get into a boat and go ahead of Him to the other side. Do you think Jesus knew what they were going to face? Absolutely! Yet, He still sent them out. Sometime in the early hours of the morning, Jesus approached the boat that was being tossed about. He was walking on the water. Mark 6 has a parallel passage account of the incident. The end of verse 48 says, "He was about to pass by them."

For many years, when I read that verse, it bothered me. I thought it meant that Jesus was going to walk on by and not help. That didn't sound like Jesus. Then I learned that the phrase is used in the Greek translation of the Old Testament when God was revealing Himself to people. God passed by Moses in order to reveal His majesty to him

(Exodus 33:18–19). Elijah had a similar encounter with the Lord (1 Kings 19:11).

Both men had the privilege of having the Lord pass by them in order to reveal His majesty and prepare them for a further purpose. That's what God did for the disciples that night, and that's what God wants to do in our lives when we encounter storms.

When the disciples saw Jesus walking on the water, they were terrified. Jesus immediately told them, "Take courage! It is I. Don't be afraid" (Matthew 14:27). Notice how quickly He acted in response to their fear. He didn't let them sit and stew in their panic.

Jesus told them to take courage because He was there. When He told them, "It is I," He was telling them the same thing God told Moses when Moses wanted to know how to identify God to the children of Israel. Exodus 3:14 says, "God said to Moses, 'I AM WHO I AM.' This is what you are to say to the Israelites: 'I AM has sent me to you.'"

When I heard that explanation, I was so excited! That reflects the loving character of God. He would never walk by and not help us when we're in trouble. He is ever present, ready to help. He wants us to look to Him and to trust Him to take care of us. Jeremiah 17:7 says, "But blessed is the man who trusts in the LORD . . . ."

I love Peter's response to Jesus walking on the water. Peter told Jesus to ask him to come to Him if it was really Jesus. Jesus told Peter to come.

Imagine how Peter must have felt when he left the boat and was actually walking on the water. What do you think he was thinking? What do you think the other disciples were thinking as they watched their friend? While I don't know what Peter or the other disciples were thinking, I do have a strong suspicion that the Lord was thrilled with Peter's faith, short-lived as it was.

Jesus told Peter to come to Him, and Peter stepped off the boat in faith. There was no hesitation in him; he recognized the voice of Jesus. When his feet took him from the boat to the sea, he was walking on faith.

God desires that people trust Him. In fact, it's impossible to please Him without faith (Hebrews 11:6). He delights in helping those who rely on Him by faith.

One moment Peter was actually walking on water; the next moment, he began to sink. What made the difference? "But when he saw the wind, he was afraid . . ." (Matthew 14:30). Peter took his eyes off Jesus and looked at the storm around him. When he took his focus off the God of the storm and focused instead on the storm itself, his faith faltered and he sank. It's important that we remember to keep our eyes on God no matter how loudly the storm around us beckons our attention with its tumultuous sounds.

Peter's faith may have left him for the moment, but he knew what to do about it. First, let's look at what he didn't do. He didn't reach down with his toes to see if he could touch the bottom. He didn't start floating or attempt to swim back to the boat. He didn't do anything to try to save himself. Instead, as soon as he began to sink, he cried out to the Lord to save him.

We need to cry out to the Lord as well. Not just for salvation, but for everyday living. It's easy to get caught up in trusting ourselves to solve problems and make things happen, but God wants us to depend on Him.

Notice how quickly Jesus responded to Peter's cry for help. Matthew 14:31 says, "Immediately Jesus reached out his hand and caught him. 'You of little faith,' he said, 'why did you doubt?'" Jesus didn't allow Peter to go under the water before He responded to his request. He immediately rescued him.

Sometimes when I've wrestled with trusting God, I've felt as if I belong to "The Little Faith Club." I bet Peter felt embarrassed in front of the Lord, and disappointed in himself for doubting. Sometimes I think of the Lord asking me the same question, "Why did you doubt?" Then I ask myself the same question.

In spite of my faltering faith at times, God has used the experiences of seeing how He worked previously in my life to strengthen my faith to face future situations. He uses the lessons learned about His faithful character to replace the seeds of doubt with seeds of faith.

The faith I'm talking about isn't just faith itself, for faith's sake. We don't merely need faith. The faith we must have is faith in Jesus. We need to recognize who He is, the great I AM, none other than God Himself.

When Jesus and Peter climbed into the boat, the wind died down and the disciples responded by worshiping Jesus. When we see Jesus for who He is, we too should respond in worship.

One other aspect of this account that is fascinating is the use of the word "immediately" in the verses. We see Jesus doing something immediately three times. He made the disciples get in the boat immediately (Matthew 14:22). He immediately responded to the disciples when they cried out in fear (v. 27), and He immediately reached out His hand to catch Peter when Peter cried out, "Lord, save me!" (vv. 30–31).

We love it when Jesus does things immediately, don't we? I sure do! Sometimes that's how He works. When it accomplishes His purposes, He acts immediately. Those are the easy times to handle.

What about when He doesn't act immediately, such as when He allowed the disciples to be out in the storm for a while? That isn't so easy to deal with, is it? In the midst of the storm, remember that Jesus is the God of the universe and that He's in sovereign control of the timing of the answers to our prayers.

God cannot be contained. Yet, there have been times when I've found myself trying to put Him in a box.

Let me explain. Have you ever thought you knew how a situation should play itself out? Have you ever thought something had to happen a certain way? Have you ever tried to talk God into taking a specific course of action because you just knew that was the right way to go? Have you ever thought He was going to do something and thought you were following Him, only to have things turn out totally differently, and you were left feeling bewildered and unsettled? I have.

Don't forget that He is God, and we are not. Even when we think we know what is best in a given situation, the truth is, only He knows the whole story. We often define everything by the moment and by what is happening right now. Instead, we need to define it by the big picture—creation through eternity.

When we're tempted to try to put God in a box, we must remember that He sees the beginning from the end. He alone knows what is best, and He alone has the ability to bring good out of bad. We may think we're wise enough to know what's best for us, but we don't know as much as we think we do. Even in situations in which we think we have all the pertinent facts and information, we don't know it all. Only God knows everything.

He can see the other side of the tapestry. We need to trust Him to use whatever dark threads He introduces as a beautiful part of what He's weaving.

During our missionary internship at West Side, Eric and I applied to a mission board, which is an organization that oversees and assists missionaries. That organization didn't have missionaries working in Peru, so we were appointed to go to Barbados, in the West Indies.

Despite my chronic fatigue syndrome, we visited many churches in the Northeast to raise the needed financial support, a process called deputation. One meeting stands out as a testimony of God's intervening power, followed by Him withdrawing it.

When we arrived, we discovered I was going to have to project my voice for the slide show without the aid of a microphone. Under normal circumstances, that wouldn't have been a problem, but I had laryngitis. We asked God to intervene.

When I began speaking, my voice was normal. For the entire presentation, I spoke without strain and projected my voice effortlessly. The moment the slides were done, I took a drink of water. When I next spoke, the laryngitis had returned.

While I was glad God had given me my voice when I needed it, I quickly changed focus and became frustrated. I said, *Lord, I appreciate You getting me through that presentation. You just showed Your power to heal my voice. Why don't You just let me have my voice back for good? It isn't too hard for You to do.*

Immediately, I was filled with remorse. Internally I recoiled, feeling as though I had slapped God in the face. He had graciously answered our prayers and had given me my voice when I needed it most. He had the prerogative to withdraw that miraculous intervention if that was His will. Who was I to tell God what to do? I asked His forgiveness and acknowledged His right to heal or not to heal in whatever timing He chose.

Many times I've found myself grappling with the reality that even though God has complete control over everything, He isn't going to use His power to act in the way I want Him to in a particular situation. At those times I have to count on the fact that He knows best, believe that He has a reason for why He's doing what He's doing, and trust His love for me, even when I don't understand.

After about two years on deputation, we learned we couldn't get work permits for Barbados, so we agreed to go to Grenada, another island in the Caribbean Sea.

My mom raised concerns about me living on a tropical island with my allergy to mold. If we had known then that the dizziness I had in Peru occurred because of my exposure to the moldy jungle environment, we would have known I couldn't live there. But we didn't.

I called our future coworkers and learned that the wife was allergic to mold. She'd done poorly in another country, but her symptoms had improved greatly while living in Grenada.

Thus reassured, we continued toward the goal of getting there. When West Side began to give missionaries from our church half their needed support, it boosted us to full support.

Early in 1990, I received medical clearance from my primary care doctor. We could hardly believe that after four long years of deputation and all our years of preparation, we were finally heading into the home stretch.

One final step was for Eric to become an ordained minister. Our church elders met with him for a lengthy session and asked him questions about a variety of topics regarding his biblical beliefs and personal relationship with God. He passed their extensive examination and was ordained. Then we threw our energies into serious packing and final preparations.

Our church family asked for a list of items we needed and everything from deodorant to disinfectant filled boxes in the church foyer due to their generosity. At home, we sorted through our belongings, stored some items at Dad and Mom's, and gave away the rest.

Benjamin spent a final week at my parents' house. They borrowed a camcorder and taped him doing all the fun things he enjoyed doing when he visited them.

Some of our family and about forty Westsiders saw us off at the airport. Many of them took time off work to be there. Even though we were sad at the thought of not seeing our dear family and friends for quite some time, we were eager to get to Grenada.

Chapter 9

Dealing with Culture Shock

HAVE YOU EVER poured your life into something because you felt God wanted you to do it, only to have "the bottom of the bag fall out" so to speak? I can tell you from personal experience that it doesn't feel good!

Have you ever allowed the pain of a circumstance to cause your relationship with the Lord to suffer? I have—and that doesn't feel too good either!

While living in Grenada, I foolishly responded to uncomfortable experiences in a wrong way. Overwhelmed by unexpected pain and lack of understanding, I allowed the circumstances and accompanying feelings to come between the Lord and me. Instead of clinging to Him, I allowed a wall to go up between us. I didn't like the wall, and I didn't want it to be there, but I didn't take it down right away either.

I'm thankful that the wall was time-limited, and that He was faithful to me when I didn't trust Him.

I want you to understand what took place so it can help you when you face disappointment, feel disillusioned, or are tempted to think less of God.

The final flight on our journey left from Puerto Rico. I was keenly aware that our years of waiting and preparing were over, and I was thankful for the privilege God was giving us. He had given us the desire to be missionaries, and He had faithfully led us on the path that had taken us to that flight, suspended between two worlds.

We were about to begin our new life. It would start the moment we touched down, or so I thought. It actually began before we landed, and it got off to a bad start.

As the plane descended, it banked sharply, allowing us to get our first glimpse of Grenada. That one look was when trouble began for me. We were so low I could see the whitecaps of the individual waves, yet I was easily able to see the entire island below us. While I had known it was small, I wasn't prepared for the reaction I had when I saw how little it looked from the air. It made me claustrophobic.

Our coworkers met us at the airport and took us to their home. Unfortunately, the location of their home made my claustrophobia worse. Grenada is very mountainous, and they lived in a narrow valley hemmed in by thick foliage.

Thus began a mental game I had to play to offset my "islanditis," as I later learned it's been called by many people. When the claustrophobia increased, I would picture a small soccer field I'd seen, the flat area near the airport, or the fields surrounding my parents' home.

One day I thought, *Okay, if this island is so small, then why don't I walk all the way around it?* Instantly I thought of my CFS and responded, *I could never do that. It's too big.* Then I told myself, *If this island is too big for me to walk around, then it's big enough!* Strangely, that impromptu argument with myself alleviated my islanditis more than anything else I tried.

As with any move to a foreign country, there were adjustments to be made. We had been taught about culture shock during candidate school, and I thought I was prepared to go through its stages. Unfortunately, my claustrophobia thrust me right into the second stage, almost totally bypassing the first, which is the "tourist stage" when everything is novel and exciting. The second stage is when the newness wears off and the reality of the cultural differences and one's need to adjust to them kicks in. That's when one begins to work through and reconcile the differences he or she views as being negative aspects of living there. It's the hardest stage of culture shock. The fact that I went into that stage first, along with my inevitable intense homesickness, made what I went through in the months ahead all the more distressing.

We found a rental house that had a ground-floor basement and garage with the living space on the second floor. We eagerly envisioned using the garage area as a gathering place for youth to play games. We planned to fix up the dilapidated bathroom and turn the extra space in the lower level into bedrooms to host missions teams. It was with great anticipation that we moved in and began to make it our home.

I soon realized that I knew more about Peru and its culture than I did about Grenada. I didn't know proper protocol, and I didn't want to offend people by accident.

The fact that it is an English-speaking country added to my dilemma. Hearing English spoken subtly planted the idea that the social customs should be the same as those I had left behind. However, something as simple as the need to pass by people on the sidewalk left me unsure of what to do. I didn't know whether to go to the right side or the left. After all, they drove on the left side of the road instead of the right.

When a neighbor had a new roof put on, I wanted to give the workmen a drink, but I didn't know if it would be considered forward if I offered them a simple drink of water. That was one mistake I didn't want to make, so I reluctantly dismissed the idea.

There were environmental differences. The climate was hot and humid. Each time Eric cut the lawn, he'd have white salt stains on his shirt by the time he was done. Our foam mattress gave off a strong foul odor from the imbedded sweat of previous tenants.

Creatures new to us affected daily life. The biting ants in our yard happened to be very prolific and aggressive. Eric had to tuck the end of his pants into his socks when he mowed the lawn or suffer the consequences of painful bites. With my love of the outdoors, having the yard essentially off limits was a huge adjustment.

Poisonous scorpions inflict a painful sting. Centipedes grow to be as thick as a pencil and several inches long. Their bite is enough to send an adult to the hospital for pain relief.

I had heard of cockroaches before, but I had no idea there are huge ones that can fly! Neither did Eric, so we were both startled one evening when we heard a buzzing sound followed by something landing on the wall above our heads in the living room. It looked to us like something out of a sci-fi movie!

Grenada is home to the smaller version of cockroaches as well. Eric bought a powerful insecticide and sprayed the kitchen every evening before going to bed. Each morning Benjamin had the job of sweeping up the dead ones.

It didn't take long for us to get used to the flying cockroaches, katydids, and bats coming through our house. We soon were able to identify them by the sound of their wings.

A friendly creature was the ever-present gecko, a type of lizard that walked on our walls. Most of the time they were several inches long. However, there were much larger ones that lived in foliage lining the house. They occasionally made their way inside and had a knack for surprising me in the shower.

Mosquitoes were everywhere and had free access to us since many of our windows didn't have screens. We didn't have mosquito netting for use at night, so we used a small electrical device that produced a smoky haze to deter mosquitoes. During our first weeks there, we had so many bites that our coworker once exclaimed to me, "My lands, girl! You have so many bites, you look like you have the chicken pox!"

Mosquitoes aren't only bothersome; they can also be dangerous. Not long after we arrived in Grenada, there was an outbreak of dengue fever. I became very ill with either dengue or a viral infection and was in bed for four weeks. The usual course for dengue is two weeks, but I went through a two-week extension, which sometimes happens. I used the time in bed to erase answers and shade over those words that could still be seen in the answer blanks in used ACE workbooks that had been donated to the Christian school.

With me out of commission, work around the house piled up. Mrs. Neptune, a local pastor's wife, came often to sweep the floors, which quickly became dirty with debris from palm trees. She brought juices, fruit, and other food for us. Her gentle spirit and love for our Lord made a deep impression on me. God used her to show us His love, and we appreciated her ministry to our family.

Just as I was beginning to be up and around, Eric came down with dengue and spent two weeks in bed. Benjamin escaped it, but he had his own set of health problems with recurring high fevers and rashes.

One afternoon, without warning, a thick white fog closed in on us. I couldn't see anything outside. Despite the heat, I shut whatever windows I could. I later learned the government fogged the island to kill mosquitoes. The chemicals used in Grenada are more potent than those allowed in the USA.

My health deteriorated as multiple environmental factors put a heavy load on my immune system. Mold was one factor that negatively affected my body. It was so prolific that even the inside of the dresser drawers in our bedroom smelled of it after a thorough cleaning. One day Eric pulled his black wingtip shoes out from under our bed and was surprised to find them covered with mold.

After each rain, our cement driveway looked like a green carpet had been rolled out because of the mold that grew on it. Often when it rained I felt like knives were being thrust through my head.

In order to address my increasing health problems, I visited the internist I had seen for the dengue. Between my allergies and repeat infections that occurred as my CFS responded poorly to the environment, Eric and I became regulars at his office. He was very knowledgeable, kind, and had a good sense of humor. We were grateful for God's provision of a good doctor.

Since there weren't any allergists on the island, the internist tried to get my allergies under control. Nothing worked, and my symptoms steadily grew worse.

Despite my health problems, we were busy. I was homeschooling Benjamin for kindergarten. We traveled to churches associated with our mission and met the pastors and the congregations.

The Grenadian pastors' committee had recently requested that missionaries from our agency return to assist them. The previous missionaries left the island just before the United States military collaborated with Grenadian and other Caribbean forces to overthrow the communist leadership in Grenada in the early eighties.

Our understanding had been that all the pastors on the committee wanted missionaries to return. After we arrived, we learned there were differences of opinion. It didn't take long for it to become fairly clear which pastors were glad to have us there and which ones were not happy about the situation.

Eric began to organize the administrative aspects of establishing a Bible Institute. It offered evening classes, since most people worked during the day and depended upon taxis for transportation. Some of the pastors allowed him to use their facilities, and classes began in three locations.

He thoroughly enjoyed preparing for his classes as well as teaching. Many nights Eric stayed late to answer questions and develop relationships with his students. We were eager to build upon the budding friendships.

The nights Eric taught, Benjamin and I stayed home. Apparently people observing our property thought that when the car was missing it meant nobody was home. By virtue of our US citizenship, we were a natural target for thieves.

While Eric was gone one evening, Benjamin and I were playing a board game after dark. We heard people quietly talking in our back yard but couldn't see them even when we shined a flashlight out the window.

That night was just the first in what became a pattern of hearing voices in the yard the nights Eric was away. When they continued to come, even though they knew I was there, I wondered what their intentions were. Benjamin and I talked about how to handle potential situations should they ever arise. I knew that the worst time for them to break in would be when the electricity wasn't working, which happened on a regular basis.

One night the electricity went off while Eric was away. I lit some candles and set them on the dining-room table and kept a flashlight nearby. A while later I heard a noise that sounded like a ladder being put against the back of the house. I went into the study and hesitated a moment before I shined the flashlight out the window. I fully expected to see someone trying to look in. With a sigh of relief, I relaxed when I didn't see anyone.

The following morning, Eric and I went out back to investigate. There were marks in the ground and on the wall where our ladder had been propped up to the right of the study window. With dismay, I realized that someone had been there the night before. Since I hadn't looked that far to the side, I hadn't seen anyone.

Another night, Benjamin and I played Monopoly at the dining-room table. Suddenly I heard a familiar metallic noise. Fear flooded through me as I identified it as the sound made by contact with the decorative cast iron railing on the veranda. I realized it meant someone was coming over the railing, and would be in the house any moment if I didn't shut the double doors.

As I sprinted across the slippery parquet floor, I saw a flash of color. A man already had his leg over the railing and was one move away from heaving the rest of his body onto the veranda. I grabbed for the right door handle, and slammed it as I simultaneously groped for the left door, transfixed by the scene in front of me.

The intruder grunted as he reversed his direction and began to back off the railing. He disentangled his leg and pulled it over the top. I heard him drop to the ground as I shut the other door.

After locking it, I ran to the window overlooking our driveway, trying to figure out what to expect next. The moment I looked out the window, I was startled by the appearance of another intruder directly below me. He fled out of the garage and raced down the driveway behind the first man. A third one emerged and followed the others. After they were out of sight, I investigated as much of the outside as I could see from each window. I didn't see or hear anyone. About every five minutes, I walked through the house listening and looking out the windows. I was afraid the men would regroup and come back. I knew the flimsy door to the small balcony off our bedroom was the most vulnerable entry point. It would be a simple task for them to get in there.

With the veranda doors closed, it quickly grew hot inside. We were very uncomfortable in the stifling heat, but I was too afraid to risk opening the doors for even a moment. For Benjamin's sake, I tried to appear calmer than I felt. In reality, my body was on high alert. I was so tense that it felt as though every muscle in me was poised to spring into action at the slightest hint of sound. At times, my heartbeat pounded so loudly in my ears that I feared I would miss hearing something. The minutes ticked by and grew into hours as I made my rounds and waited for the sound of our car coming up the driveway.

When Eric got home and opened the door, he immediately felt the increased temperature and looked at us quizzically. He set his briefcase down and asked us why we had the place all closed up.

After what we'd been through, the sight of him reopening the veranda doors made me uneasy, even though I knew there probably wasn't anything to fear. The cool night breeze flowed through the open doorway as we told him what happened.

The following day, Eric went to a neighboring pastor's home to buy eggs. Eric told him what had been happening at our house. As it turned out, the pastor had a son-in-law who lived about a mile from us. He was a policeman, but he worked in a different precinct than ours. The pastor talked with him and then gave us his son's home phone number and his number at the police station. The son-in-law said to call him if anything else transpired, because it would be quicker for him to get to our house, even from his police station, than it would be for us to get help from our precinct. He also said he would do what he could to put an end to our problem.

From that day on, we were left alone. He put the word out on the street that we were to be left alone, or else! Apparently, the "or else" part wasn't something anyone wanted to experience! We were grateful to the Lord for His protection and for providing a solution to our problem.

Chapter 10

Allowing a Wall to Go Up

EVENTS IN GRENADA were definitely not unfolding the way we expected—or wanted them to. My allergies continued to get worse. We investigated other options for treatment. One idea was for me to go back to the States for allergy testing and get started on shots. Once stabilized, I could return to Grenada.

We called Carol Cassara, and she looked into the possibility. A doctor she spoke with was skeptical that my allergies could be brought under control in a short time. Plus, even if he was successful in reining them in, I would need to have an allergist in Grenada who could administer shots, monitor progress, do further testing, and prepare new serum as necessary. We already knew there were no allergists on the island. On a long shot, we asked the internist if he could do it for me, but it required specialized training he didn't have.

While we waited to see what would happen with my allergies, we continued to have opportunities to minister to others. One of the opportunities came about in a very unusual way.

One day Mom called and asked me to pray for my cousin. He had taken an overdose, then changed his mind and called for help.

Within a week, God used that news to open the way for us to reach out to one of our neighbors. This particular neighbor was another one of the pastors associated with our mission. He had kept his distance from us. We didn't know why, but guessed he was one of the pastors who didn't want missionaries back.

One day we learned that his wife's brother had committed suicide, so we went over to their house. The pastor was out front chopping wood. Eric stayed with him, and I was invited to sit with his wife inside. I expressed our condolences, and she said a couple of sentences telling me what I already knew. I listened and then told her about my cousin's attempted suicide. My voluntary revelation was a sort of battering ram on the invisible wall between us. Her entire countenance changed, and she opened up and began talking. As I listened, I felt the gap between us being bridged.

While we talked inside, Eric was having a similar experience with the pastor in the front yard. They discovered some misunderstandings that had come out of the men's committee meetings. The pastor had come to some incorrect conclusions about the views our coworker held. From there, he had assumed Eric held the same views. He was relieved to learn the truth, and they had a good conversation.

During the short walk home, we rejoiced in what God had accomplished. Isaiah 55 tells us that God's thoughts are not our thoughts, and our ways are not His ways. I wouldn't have thought He would bring good out of someone's attempted suicide, but God works in unexpected ways.

There were lots of things happening that I hadn't expected, and I was having a hard time dealing with some of them.

Eric and I were on totally different pages in our emotional responses to the culture shock. He was in the initial tourist stage and was enamored with everything. I was less than enamored, to put it mildly.

I longed to take the initiative in developing relationships, but had been told that the culture required me to wait for them to approach me first. I felt trapped by a social custom that went against my grain as a people person. My frustration heightened when I learned that one of our neighbors thought I was the coldest person she had ever met.

Our family continued to have health problems, and they were wearing me down physically, mentally, and emotionally. I spent so much time at the doctor's office that we began to interact on a friendly basis. In addition to my bout with dengue, infections, and my allergy problems, my CFS was getting worse in the heat and humidity.

Minor irritants were magnified in size by everything else. Our refrigerator repeatedly broke down and didn't get fixed for weeks at a time. Our PVC water pipes lay exposed on the ground outside, and we didn't have a water heater, so we had cold showers in the morning when we wanted a warm shower and hot showers in the afternoon when we wanted to cool off.

Our coworkers suggested we go to the beach to relax and rejuvenate. The water was warm and clear, and I enjoyed swimming until I saw a water snake under me. We were told it was poisonous. That ended my swim.

A bat wedged itself between two sheets of plywood in the bathroom ceiling and died. We could see part of it, but we couldn't get it out. It took weeks for the stench to dissipate.

For a while, we had to sit sideways and keep our legs out from under the dining-room table in order not to get bitten by sand fleas. It was amazing how such little creatures could make something as simple as eating a bowl of cereal a challenge.

Eric had the worst time with sand fleas. When he began to get bites on his backside from his waist down, we couldn't figure out where he was being exposed to them. Benjamin and I weren't having the problem. We finally realized he was getting bitten when he was in our car driving to his Bible Institute classes. That explained why he was the only one who was getting bitten, and the specific area of his body affected. One night I counted his bites. He had 108 bites on his backside between his waist and his ankles.

By that point, I was beginning to think that God had saved all the nasty creatures He didn't know what to do with at creation and placed them all on the island of Grenada!

The lack of ability to sit on our lawn and enjoy the out-of-doors was a huge adjustment for me. I loved being outside and had spent much of my childhood living in the country. The cooped-up feeling fed into my islanditis, and made the culture shock worse.

The knowledge that some of the pastors didn't want us there weighed heavily on me. I tried to offset it with thoughts of the pastors who were glad we were there.

One of the biggest problems I faced was being isolated. My extended time with the dengue fever was to blame for my initial isolation, but even after I was on my feet again, aside from church services, I had limited contact with people except our coworkers and one neighbor. I wanted to meet people and have an active part in ministry.

Homesickness was another problem. I knew the intense feelings would eventually subside, and I longed for the inner relief that would bring.

These are some of the factors that chipped away at my internal world. Most of them weren't big enough to seriously rock my boat all by themselves. However, we don't always face uncomfortable issues one at a time, do we? Sometimes we're inundated with a host of smaller factors that have a snowball effect and emerge as a huge force. That's the situation I was in.

It's easy to feel close to the Lord when things are going well, isn't it? But what happens when things don't turn out as you thought they were going to? What do you do then?

As you'll see, I blew it in Grenada. Instead of staying close to the Lord and clinging to Him, I allowed a wall to go up between us. I still talked to Him and counted on Him for certain things, but our relationship wasn't the same. The tender intimacy and confident reliance upon Him that I normally enjoyed was marred by an undercurrent of confusion, discomfort, unsettledness, and my lack of understanding.

Watch out when you find yourself in similar situations in life! Guard your heart when you are hurting and restless. At those times, we're extremely vulnerable to Satan's attack. He's smart too. He knows just how to weasel in and where to strike his blow to cause the most damage.

In my case, he attacked subtly and quietly with my thoughts, silently undermining my confidence in the Lord and my dependence on Him. Be careful, because he'll attempt to do the same thing to you. The life circumstances he'll use won't be the same as mine, but his end goal is the same. He wants to drive a wedge between you and God.

Are you going through something right now that's causing you to wonder about the Lord? To doubt His love, or His commitment to you; to cause your relationship with Him not to be quite as close as it once was?

Don't let Satan trick you! Take time to clear the air between you and God, and don't let anything, or anyone, get between the two of you like I did in Grenada.

As time went on, I was aware that something was different in my relationship with the Lord. I still prayed, but I didn't feel the same inside. On the one hand, I knew He was with me, and I appreciated seeing Him at work in some wonderful ways. Yet I could tell our relationship wasn't the same.

I had waited most of my life to be on the mission field, and now I was there. Only, things hadn't turned out like I thought they were going to. All the years of waiting, preparing, and anticipation had culminated in me being on the mission field in inner turmoil. Everywhere I looked, things had turned out differently. I wanted God to take away the culture shock, and I wished He hadn't allowed me to go right into the second stage of it instead of taking the normal path like Eric had.

I was disappointed with God for allowing what was going on in my life. The fact that I couldn't allow myself to acknowledge disappointment with God only complicated matters as I attempted to deal with the reality of it, but I also sidestepped calling it by that name. It became my "elephant in the room." I had very strong feelings about what I thought God wasn't doing for me and about what He had allowed me to face; yet, I didn't talk to Him about my feelings toward Him. I only talked with Him about other, "safer" areas of my life. On a growing basis, I felt a coolness developing in our relationship that was born out of my emerging uncertainty about Him. I was unsure of what He would and wouldn't do for me, and I increasingly felt on my own.

I eventually realized I felt a sense of betrayal. Although I had known there would be struggles and adjustments when we arrived in Grenada, I hadn't expected to have such a hard time handling them.

Despite our training in culture shock, I was unprepared for the emotional upheaval accompanying it. Physical problems, such as the lack of screens to keep out mosquitoes, could be seen with the eye and objectively evaluated. The worst aspects of the culture shock I experienced dealt with subjective issues that couldn't be seen but were just as powerful.

My inner turmoil mounted. None of the issues were getting resolved. New ones kept arising and adding themselves to the growing pot that stirred within me. Looking back, not having someone to talk things over with curtailed my progress in dealing with the culture shock.

Normally, the Lord was my primary source of help. However, because I wasn't relating to Him on the same intimate basis I was used to, I effectively shut out the One I needed. Eric was willing to listen, but he had no basis of experience to enable him to understand. Since I wasn't receiving help from the two sources I normally relied on, I felt alone as I tried to gain a solid emotional footing.

One day while working in the kitchen, I was overwhelmed by my poor health, the relentless heat, and the inner aching. I started talking out loud to the Lord. I expressed my dislike at living there and asked Him to take us back to the States. Even as I spoke, I knew that leaving wasn't what I wanted. What I really desired was to be relieved of the intense pain, adjusted to the environment, healthy, and actively involved in the ministry. At that moment, I didn't see how it could happen.

One evening, my good friend in Rochester, Lin Lohman, called to see how we were doing. The familiar sound of her voice and her compassionate concern released the gate of my pent-up feelings. I leaned against the cement wall in the hallway and allowed a flood of negative emotions to pour out of my mouth and into the phone. She listened as I gave her a detailed account of many of the troubling issues I was facing. I ended by saying, "I just can't believe it, Lin. After all the years of preparation and looking forward to it, I can't believe I'm here and that I hate it."

When I finally stopped my monologue, she responded, "I'm so sorry, Maureen."

Her words were a gift from God. She allowed me to voice my feelings without condemning me, and she expressed her sorrow. She is a faithful prayer warrior, and I was comforted to know that she would be praying for me in very specific ways.

Her phone call enabled me to set aside some of my frustrations and gain some emotional space inside. I realized that much of my problem stemmed from false expectations. I had anticipated having to deal with issues but was blindsided by the ones that had arisen. I was taken off guard by the fact that I felt the way I did and that everything was turning out so differently than I expected. This had left me asking, *Why are You allowing me to go through this, God? I thought I knew what to expect and had prepared well enough to get through anything.*

As I thought things through, I realized I needed to focus on the fact that "this too shall pass." As troubling as they were, given time, my reactions and uncomfortable experiences with culture shock would be dealt with and the pain would fade away. Just as my homesickness always gave me a run for my money before it subsided, the culture shock was doing the same thing.

I needed to change my expectations and deal with whatever came my way instead of being so shocked that I had to deal with issues I hadn't anticipated. I still didn't know how it would happen, but I felt comforted in the knowledge that it would work out.

I began to get my focus off the pain of not understanding what He was allowing to happen and back on Him and the fact that He would see me through it.

The wall I had put up started to crumble.

Chapter 11

Losing a Dream in Grenada

MY ALLERGIES NEEDED to be addressed by a specialist, so the internist arranged for me to see an ear, nose, and throat (ENT) specialist who came in from Barbados once a month. We were eager to see him and get my allergies under control.

After his exam, he sat down behind his desk and faced us. We waited expectantly. He looked at Eric somberly and said, "I don't know what it was that caused you to bring your family to this island in the first place, but you have a decision to make. You're going to have to decide if it's important enough to stay, because if you stay here, your wife will go deaf."

Shock, disbelief, and a flood of emotions swept through my mind. *What? Deaf? Leave Grenada? What's he talking about? How can that be possible? There has to be something that can be done!*

Eric asked some questions, and my thoughts came back into focus. The doctor explained what was wrong. My ears were retaining fluid because of the moldy environment. The perpetual fluid retention was putting pressure on my eardrums and damaging them. Over time, they would become increasingly less taut until it got to the point where they could no longer perform, resulting in deafness.

We asked if there was anything that could be done there or in the States to control it so that deafness wouldn't occur. He said the only answer to avoid deafness was for me to leave the island. Numbly, we thanked him for seeing us and left.

Although we knew my allergy problem was serious, neither of us had been prepared to hear what he had said. We didn't want to believe it was true, even though it perfectly fit the picture. It explained why Dad and Mom always had to be careful about where our family lived while I was growing up, and why I became dizzy in Peru after being out on the river boat. My body can't tolerate living near water or being exposed to the mold that flourishes in damp conditions.

In the midst of my jumbled thoughts, I was amazed to realize the transforming effect the news was having on my internal struggles. Faced with the prospect of actually having to leave, I began viewing things differently than I had. It somehow gave me the ability to extract myself from the draining intensity of my ongoing battle with the culture shock and allowed me to view the entire scenario from a completely different position than previously had been possible.

The day I had talked to the Lord in the kitchen, I had felt it would take forever, if it was even possible, to work through the culture shock, adjust, and be involved in ministry. Then, as a result of my phone call with Lin, I'd been encouraged that, given time, it would work out. I just didn't have any idea how that was going to happen. Now, the ENT's pronouncement jolted me hard enough that I was finally able to not only know it could work out but also to envision how some of it could take place—if only we could stay.

The thought of actually leaving was something neither of us could comprehend. Even though it seemed like the decision was a no-brainer, for us it wasn't that simple. Emotionally, we clung to the ability to be there. I didn't want to give it up; neither did Eric.

The responsibility for making such an important decision weighed heavily on Eric's shoulders. He called our mission headquarters and West Side. Everyone was sympathetic with our predicament, but nobody was willing to come right out and tell him what to do.

I'd never seen Eric agonize so much over a decision. The sorrow, pain, and inner turmoil he felt were reflected in his eyes. I knew he needed to talk to someone who would listen, understand his feelings, and actually advise him. Deep down, Eric already knew what we should do, but he desperately needed someone to verbally confirm his decision and give him emotional permission to leave. There was only one person I felt could give Eric what he needed. That person was his dad.

At the time, his parents were missionaries in Kenya. I said, "Eric, you need to talk to your dad. I don't care how much money it costs, just call your dad."

Eric talked to his dad for thirty minutes. When he hung up, I could tell from his eyes that he finally had his decision made. Internally, I thanked the Lord for allowing Eric to get to talk to his dad and for the fact that the conversation obviously met Eric's need to talk it out and enabled him to make a decision. Even though neither of us liked the conclusion, he said we would leave.

We began a whirlwind of activity in order to arrange for Benjamin and me to leave as quickly as possible. We purchased tickets for the following week's flight back to the States. Since Eric was only part way through teaching his Bible Institute courses, he decided to stay an additional six weeks to complete the term before he joined us.

We sorted through our belongings and packed suitcases. There were several wedding presents and a guitar that I didn't want to part with but had to leave behind. Eric wanted to take as little as possible back to the States because of the cost.

Of all that transpired that final week, one of the most special moments took place when the neighboring pastor and his wife were visiting us. During the conversation, he said, "I still have not come to accept the fact that you have to leave." My heart swelled with gratitude to the Lord for bridging the gap that had once separated us.

All too soon, the day arrived for Benjamin and me to leave Grenada on an afternoon flight. Eric surprised me by picking up one of my favorite meals for lunch. I didn't get to eat too much of it in between people stopping by to say a final farewell.

Before we left for the airport, I walked through the house one last time, pausing a moment in each room, trying to imprint each detail in my memory.

Lord, it seems as though we just got here. I remember trying to decide where to store things. Now we have to go. I'm thankful for the time You allowed us to be here. I just wish we could have stayed. I don't want to leave, Lord! Do we really have to?

As I walked down the steps for the final time, I was acutely aware that every motion moved me along in a process I didn't want to go through. It was happening too fast. I wanted time to slow down. I twisted my body and stared back up at the house as we went down the driveway. As Eric pulled onto the road, I strained for a last glimpse.

That's my home! I don't want to leave and never come back! Can't we call it off and at least let me stay longer? The doctor said it would take a while for me to go deaf. Maybe we can ask him how long he thinks I could stay before the damage would be too great. Can't we talk this over? I'm not ready to leave yet!

I tried to see everything on the way to the airport. Memories of events that had taken place in my short time there replayed in my mind. My emotions were bouncing around all over the place.

Stop the car! Can't we please turn around and go back? I don't want to leave these people! All our dreams for ministering here for the rest of our lives are over. This doesn't make sense! Why am I in a car going back to the airport? We weren't supposed to do that for four years. Why is this happening? Eric and I won't ever get the chance to reach out to people the way we dreamed of doing. Isn't that what You wanted us to do? Now our house won't be a gathering place, and we'll never host missions teams.

I dreaded being separated from Eric for so long, and I wondered how I would get through the trip without his help. *I don't want to leave Eric! I miss him already, and we haven't even left yet! How am I going to manage getting four suitcases and our carry-on bags through customs by myself?*

I regretted my emotional response to the culture shock, and the distance I had put between the Lord and me. *I'm sorry for letting the wall go up between us, Lord! I wish I had handled the culture shock better!*

My mind whirled around a nagging fear, and my insides churned because of the possibility of it being true.

I'm sorry, Lord! Please forgive me! I didn't really want to go back when I talked to You that day in the kitchen. What I really wanted was to be well-adjusted to life here and to be healthy and involved in ministry. You know my heart, Lord. I asked You to take us back only because at that moment I didn't think it was possible for me to get to that point. Lord, do we have to leave because of what I said to You that day? I hope not! Is that why this is happening?

Every rotation of the tires took me past people and places I would never get to see again. I wanted to spend every moment looking out the window, trying to burn the images in my memory, but my fear demanded an answer to its question.

That doesn't make sense. It can't be the reason, because this isn't the first time I've had fluid retention because of mold. I have to leave because of a previously known problem, not because I told the Lord I wanted to go home. If we had known how much mold there was, we would have known I couldn't live here and we wouldn't have come in the first place.

That knowledge helped my conscience but did nothing to soothe the pain of leaving. *Why did it have to turn out this way? What are we going to do now, Lord? We didn't have any other plans but this one.*

Once again, I was suspended between two lives. Four and a half months earlier, I'd been eager to begin our new life in Grenada. I was full of ideas, curious, excited to get there and to experience everything and thankful for the opportunity and privilege of serving as missionaries for the rest of our lives. I had a purpose for being on that plane. It was the culmination of many years of preparation, and I was ready to get started.

Now, I had to leave and couldn't come back, and I regretted many things that had taken place. I was full of questions, and had no idea what we were going to do. I felt as if I had disappointed the Lord and had made a mess of things during the time I had been there. The many years of preparation had been for such a short time. It was over before I really got started. I was going to board a plane and go back, but to what? What was our purpose now? Where were we supposed to go, and what were we supposed to do?

As we approached the ticket counter at the airport, we were surprised to see a family we had met at Thanksgiving. They were relatives of a missionary serving with another organization and were visiting for the holiday. They were supposed to have left for the States the previous day, but their plane had a mechanical problem and the airline had to fly someone down from the USA to fix it. They were leaving on the same flight as Benjamin and I, and offered to look out for us.

I could hardly believe my ears. *Wow, God! You had a planeload of people spend an extra night in Grenada just for me!* It was an awesome answer to prayer and an unmistakable display of God's love for me.

We hugged Eric and walked across the tarmac to the waiting plane. Our friends were seated a few rows behind us.

When we arrived in Puerto Rico, we were informed that we would be going through customs there instead of in the US as I had anticipated. The family divided up our suitcases and carried them to the customs checkpoint. The officials allowed them to pass through with me in order to carry the suitcases. All I was responsible for were our carry-on bags. After depositing our suitcases, they said good-bye and went back to go through customs for themselves.

There was only one more hurdle I had to cross. I needed to find our departure gate. As we got closer to our destination, the surroundings began to become vaguely familiar to me. When I saw the gate, I broke into a huge grin. It was the gate we had used on our way to Grenada. As we sank into the same seats we had sat in then, I was very aware of God's watch-care over us. His love and attention to the details of my life were overwhelming!

When the plane landed in Syracuse, New York, Benjamin and I were greeted by my parents and our good friend, Tony Cassara. Tony was on a business trip and arranged to be at the airport in case we needed his trunk space to haul our suitcases. It was a good thing he was there, because we wouldn't have been able to fit everything into the car.

As we drove along the thruway for the hour-and-a-half ride to Rochester, I could hardly peel my eyes away from the passing snow-covered fields. Being able to see a distant, continuing landscape caused a soothing, freeing feeling to wash over me. I was startled by the dramatic change taking place as I drank in the sight of expansive open areas. For the first time since I had looked out the plane window and was immediately subjected to the constricting, suffocating grip characteristic of islanditis, I felt the claustrophobic knot begin to unwind.

Dad and Mom spent the night at the Cassaras's with us. Since I needed to see doctors in Rochester, Benjamin and I stayed behind when my parents returned to Pennsylvania.

At West Side, many people greeted me and assured me of their prayer support. Others called me at the Cassaras's house to touch base. Thankfully, of all the phone calls I received while I was there, only one left me troubled and unsettled. The caller asked what Eric and I were going to do and told me I needed to get a job. He suggested I could apply at a local grocery chain that was advertising for workers.

I didn't know how to respond. I hadn't worked outside the home before we went to Grenada. I wondered why he thought I would do so now, especially in the condition I was in with my allergies and CFS. As far as wanting to know what we were going to do next, nobody wanted to know the answer to that question more than Eric and I. I was relieved when the call ended.

Carol had been at the kitchen sink while I was on the phone. Knowing me so well, she could tell I was troubled, and she asked what was wrong. I told her what had been said. She came over and gave me a hug. Then she helped me gain a better understanding of what the call probably represented. Even though I still stung inside, I felt considerably better after our talk and was grateful for Carol's wisdom and compassion.

John and Lin Lohman invited me to their house one evening, and they listened as I talked about Grenada. They gave me a great gift that night as they allowed me to share many reflections and tell them some of the things that had taken place. Because I hadn't been gone very long and my health was the common focal point of people's inquiries, the ministry aspect of being in Grenada wasn't usually the topic that arose in conversation. I felt a need to talk about the experiences I had been through, both good and bad. Strangely enough, I found myself beginning to identify with what Eric had experienced as I went through a type of delayed first-stage of culture shock. That response, which had so effectively eluded me while there, now spontaneously took root within me. Seemingly out of nowhere, I found many things to be enamored with as I looked back with longing. During the hours I talked, they patiently listened as I kept changing the dark lenses through which I had viewed Grenada most of my time there to the newly emerging rose-tinted ones—and back again. They took it all in stride.

On a daily basis, my insides were a turbulent mass of mixed emotions, continually churning about, as though caught in an internal, invisible washing machine. Thoughts and feelings kept being thrust down and reappearing moments later, only to repeat the process. Each one surfaced long enough to be recognized and felt, but was swept under once again before it could be addressed. I was caught in a world of bewilderment, pain, uncertainty, and sorrow. My fragile spirit vainly tried to gain a foothold on the shifting surface beneath me. I felt like a ship in distress, in search of a safe harbor where I could dock for much-needed repairs.

Questions plagued my mind, rudely demanding answers I couldn't give. *Where am I supposed to begin in the necessary process of dealing with all that happened to us? How am I supposed to find time to deal with that when there are so many daily demands? What about our future? What will we do? Will a real person ever pick up the phone at the IRS and answer my multitude of questions about our tax liability now that we had returned? How can I help Benjamin get over the trauma caused by the intruders?* (Whenever he saw people wearing knit caps, he thought they were robbers.) *When will I begin to see a decrease in my symptoms? What will the doctor find? How is Eric getting along? Will my world ever calm down? How long will it be before I feel a sense of settled direction and purpose again?*

The only doctor I could see quickly was my primary care doctor. He was sad that my health had deteriorated so much and referred me to an allergist. As is often the case with specialists, my appointment wasn't for several weeks, so we went to live with my parents until Eric returned.

As I settled into my new routine, I tried to deal with the intense pain and sense of bewilderment that plagued me. I had so many unanswered questions about what had taken place and almost as many questions about our uncertain future.

In the days, weeks, and even months that followed, I attempted to come to an understanding that would make some sense of what had happened. An uncertain, vulnerable feeling permeated my being, as I no longer had a purposeful direction in which to head. For years, everything we had done was with one purpose, to get us on the mission field. Now, I felt as though the rug had been pulled out from under me, throwing me completely off balance and causing me to grasp for something to enable me to regain my sense of direction. It was as though an integral part of me had died, and indeed it had. Where identifying purpose once existed to continually focus my energies toward a specific goal, an empty void now permeated my spirit. The overwhelming sense of loss accompanying the void created a gaping wound, painfully raw and jagged around the edges. It was not the sort of wound that would heal quickly. It was the type of deep wound that would fester and cause further pain if not attended to carefully.

A multitude of questions peppered my mind. *Why did we spend all those years preparing only to have to return months after we arrived? What was the purpose of going all the way there, when God knew I couldn't live there and would have to come right back? He knew about my allergies and what the conditions were like in Grenada. Why hadn't He allowed us to obtain a correct assessment of the mold exposure? After all, we followed up on Mom's concerns, and tried to make sure I could handle living there. What are we going to do now?*

We both still desired to be involved in ministry, but where—and when? I felt like a displaced person who didn't belong anywhere, and I didn't know what to do about it.

While I didn't have answers to my questions, I knew Who did. I was glad I could talk everything over with the One who is never taken by surprise. I didn't even know what to pray for, but He did. Romans 8:26 says, "In the same way, the Spirit helps us in our weakness. We do not know what we ought to pray for, but the Spirit himself intercedes for us with groans that words cannot express."

I don't know about you, but I usually don't like change. I'm trying to be more open to it, but my inclination still is to cling to the known. I don't like feeling uprooted and uncomfortable, and there is a measure of comfort in the familiar.

In the Book of Deuteronomy, the children of Israel faced a huge change with the anticipated transfer of power from Moses to Joshua. In chapter 31, Moses talks to them about the change in leadership that was to take place. He told them what the Lord said He would do for them in the Promised Land, and then said, "Be strong and courageous. Do not be afraid or terrified because of them, for the LORD your God goes with you; he will never leave you nor forsake you" (v. 6).

Then Moses addresses Joshua. Can you imagine how Joshua must have felt? Forty years earlier, he was one of only two spies who came back from a clandestine survey of the land and said, "Let's go for it!" At that point, Moses was right in front of him and it was Moses' job to lead them in.

All they had to do was follow God. He had promised to give them the Promised Land. So what happened? Why didn't they go in?

The other ten spies said the Israelites couldn't beat the inhabitants. They looked at the human circumstances and left God out of the picture. Instead of taking God at His Word, they didn't believe what He said. They failed to look back at what God had already done for them and instead listened to their hearts of unbelief. The rest of the people believed their negative report and grumbled against the Lord.

We read in Numbers 14:11, "The LORD said to Moses, 'How long will these people treat me with contempt? How long will they refuse to believe in me, in spite of all the miraculous signs I have performed among them?'"

Instead of receiving the good gift God wanted to give them, Israel wandered in the wilderness one year for each day the spies were in the Promised Land (14:34). Four decades later, every adult male who would have entered the Promised Land, except Moses, Joshua, and Caleb, had died. Moses was right in front of Joshua, but he wouldn't be allowed to go with them. This time it was Joshua's job to lead them in.

Moses wanted Joshua to put his trust in God's ongoing faithfulness. When he addressed Joshua about the transfer of power, he told him to be strong and of good courage because the Lord Himself would go before him and would never leave or forsake him. He told him not to be afraid or discouraged.

Notice that Moses stressed the same point to the children of Israel and their new leader when they were facing change and uncertainty. Moses wanted them to focus on the most important truth, which was that God Himself was going to go with them through whatever they faced.

When we go through hard times, there is something more important than what we're facing, and that is *who* is facing it with us. We need to cling to the *who* when the *what* makes us afraid.

The fact of His presence is another foundational truth we need to hang on to tightly. Even when we can't sense Him, He's there, because He promised to be with us always (Matthew 28:20).

I'm reminded of the anonymous words on a plaque that my good friend, Carol, gave me in 1998 when I faced a trial. It says, "Lord, help me to remember that nothing is going to happen to me today that You and I can't handle together."

When new trials come my way, I try to remember to keep focused on that truth. I've learned that having an awareness of His presence in the forefront of my mind has a calming effect on my response to situations.

My distressing experience in the wake of having to return from Grenada was the perfect opportunity for God to teach me more about Himself. In so doing, unbeknown to me, He was lovingly doing more than merely helping me get through the current crisis I was facing; He was patiently and deliberately adding to the foundation of trust in Him that He was constructing in my inner spirit. He knew future events would attempt to weaken and destroy what He was establishing.

In looking back, I'm thankful for the way God graciously used my incorrect response in Grenada for good in my life. He taught me to be careful when I face painful situations. I can either respond incorrectly, like I did then, or I can choose to trust God when life hurts.

I know what it is to allow something to affect my relationship with God in such a way as to put distance between us. I know what it is to fall for Satan's lie and to feel that God is less than who He is. I know what it is to be duped into allowing something to come between God and me—and I don't ever want to go there again.

Over the course of time, God gave me some meaningful insights into our situation. While I still didn't understand why God had allowed it to turn out that way, my focal point began to broaden. Slowly, I began to view life and what had happened differently. I mentally pictured a large chessboard with a map of North and South America on its surface. Dark lines formed a grid which covered the board.

God's hand played the game, planning and executing each move. I was a pawn on His chessboard, and He had every right to move me wherever He wanted to, even all the way to Grenada and right back again. As silly as it may sound, that analogy was a tremendous help to me.

I began to realize that as Christians we need to acknowledge God's right to bring, or allow, change in our lives. That's a whole lot easier said than done. We don't understand what criteria God uses in each case to decide when or when not to divinely intervene and prevent or reverse uncomfortable situations. We often live with the consequences of other people's actions, whether right or wrong. We also can become so accustomed to God's blessings that we expect life to always continue the same way. We can begin to take things for granted instead of having an awareness of the temporary nature of this life.

Every day God blesses us in so many ways, and we don't stop to realize that in a single moment of time the world we have experienced and enjoyed could forever change.

Although unaware of it at the time, the painful experience of having to leave Grenada was just the beginning of our family having to deal with heartbreaking events. The following years brought many more blows our way. Thankfully, we didn't have to face them alone. God was with us as the knots continued to accumulate on the underside of the tapestry.

Chapter 12

Settling into a Routine

LEAVING GRENADA WASN'T part of my plan, and much of what has transpired since then doesn't resemble what I expected my life would be.

God knows us individually, and He is working out His plan in and through us. He told Jeremiah, "Before I formed you in the womb I knew you, before you were born I set you apart" (Jeremiah 1:5). David said that all the days ordained for him were written in God's book before one of them came to be (Psalm 139:16).

It's easy to make our own plans and think we're in control of our lives. Inevitably something happens to shatter the illusion and bring us back to reality.

The forced return from Grenada was an illusion-shattering experience. In all our years of preparation, we never considered the possibility of it not working out. We felt God wanted us to be missionaries and had single-mindedly prepared for that future. Having the rug pulled out from under us put us in an emotional and situational free-fall. Our entire mental outlook revolved around career missions for so long that we had no idea where, when, or how we were going to land.

My health was in a shambles. When I saw the allergist, he told me, "Maureen, your body is like a runaway freight train. It's totally out of control. You're highly allergic to absolutely everything I tested you for." I had naively thought that my allergies would calm down and I would go back to my pre-Grenada health simply by getting out of the moldy environment, but it didn't work out that way. I had long-term problems even though we left.

While we tried to figure out what God wanted us to do next, we rented an apartment in Rochester. Eric worked on a project compiling information for manuals for our mission agency, and we investigated other fields of service. One by one, the other places were eliminated.

Eric resumed teaching Bible classes as a volunteer at an inner city Bible Institute that was part of a family mission. He enjoyed teaching and interacting with his students. Not long after he began teaching, the leaders of the mission started looking into the possibility of hiring a director for the Bible Institute and expanding that ministry.

Eric met with the three-member executive board to discuss the position. It was an excellent match for his training, spiritual gifts, and experience. The men were unanimously in favor of hiring him and said they would talk with the full board of directors.

Have you ever had a time when you thought everything was falling into place and it finally was going to make sense? That's what we thought at that point. As we reflected on what was happening, we began to feel confident that God brought us back from Grenada to have Eric be involved in that ministry. Everything seemed to fit into place, including the fact that we could stay in Rochester and not have to take a chance on me having more allergy problems in another environment.

The more we thought about it, the more excited and sure we became. It was such a good match and made so much sense! Although we still hurt from having to leave Grenada, the prospect of seeing God place us in another ministry buoyed our spirits. We felt tantalizingly close to being able to settle into a purposeful direction once again. We could barely wait to get started!

In an unbelievable turn of events, the board unanimously decided against creating the position. To have believed God was opening an opportunity and showing us what He wanted us to do, only to have it fall apart when we were that close, was a shock. We were devastated. That, along with the fact that we lost half our support when West Side took us out of the new missions budget that year, ended our search for a new ministry.

We put out a final newsletter to our prayer and financial supporters and notified them of our resignation from our mission. A few supporters generously continued to help us financially until we were able to support ourselves.

Even though we still desired to be in full-time ministry, we had to switch gears and find employment for Eric. We needed the Lord to intervene, because Eric's training and experience were in ministry and unrelated to the types of jobs for which he was applying.

While job hunting one day, Eric applied at a temporary agency. He called to tell me he had been offered a two-day job and wondered if he should take it. We decided the income would be worth the lapse in the job search.

It amazes me how God works in such little things to accomplish His purposes. The company Eric went to work for is a family owned and operated boxboard packaging plant. Specializing in high-end runs, the company offers a complete line of services beginning with design layout and ending with the ability to package the final product for shipment to stores. Eric reported to the company's sister plant, which handles the packaging process, and he attached coupons to suntan lotion boxes. At the end of the second day, his boss received notification from two employees that they were quitting effective immediately, so she asked him to stay on.

It still evokes awe in me as I reflect on what God has done for us by providing that two-day temporary job. As work slowed down, Eric was the only temporary employee that was kept on. His boss asked if he would like to be hired as a full-time employee. Since we were still hoping to find a paid ministry opportunity, he declined the offer.

After a while, Eric was transferred to the main plant. Eventually, the company said it would take its chances with how long he would be there, and hired him.

Eric worked a lot of overtime and had two side jobs mowing lawns. He often left at 6:30 AM and didn't return home until 10:00 PM.

Both of us believed our family should be first priority, but we didn't know how else to provide for our financial needs. Eric was missing out on so much taking place at home with Benjamin and our new baby, Daniel, who joined us in the spring of 1993.

Eric's normally robust strength began to give out. Many nights he arrived home completely wiped out.

While difficult situations are tough at the time, they sometimes afford the perfect opportunity for us to see God use His power on our behalf. Often, circumstances worsen and get to a desperate point before God surprises us with the good He brings out of the situation.

My growing concern for Eric was not without merit. His health steadily declined, and friends began to notice the change in him. My fears were realized one day when Eric collapsed on the floor and couldn't get up.

He had developed hypoglycemia and needed a totally revised schedule. The doctor told him he was not allowed to work more than eight hours a day and must get proper food and rest. To neglect these instructions would be to invite a total physical breakdown. We didn't know how to keep that schedule and still meet our financial needs.

An unexpected phone call from an acquaintance Eric hadn't spoken with in years was an answer to prayer. He was working for a company in a town west of Rochester. They needed a production manager, and the man had thought of Eric, even though the business had nothing to do with the packaging industry.

Curious as to whether this was God's leading, Eric agreed to an initial meeting at the plant, which led to further discussions followed by a job offer. We were amazed by the generous salary and benefits they offered.

After praying and weighing our options, we decided to accept the offer. We didn't want to leave our church family and walk away from the deep roots we had put down in Rochester, but we didn't see any other way to meet our family's needs.

When Eric submitted his resignation, he was given a counter offer. That evening, Eric and I discussed the situation to try to determine what the Lord wanted us to do. Did He want us to move and was using the current situation to cause us to do so? Or was He just using that offer to cause Eric's employer to give us the counter offer? We prayed for God's guidance and compared the details of the two packages. We realized that if we subtracted the hefty travel allowance the new company was including, the salary dropped to exactly what his current employer was offering.

A closer look at the figures revealed that the increase in pay from his current employer would be the same amount Eric had been earning in his overtime pay. Eric would be able to stay at his current job, work shorter hours, and still pay our bills.

We were overwhelmed with what God had done! He used Eric's collapse to pave the way for him to get the work schedule and finances we needed. Only God has that kind of power, and it amazes me every time I see Him lovingly use it on our behalf.

There was another area of life we needed to address. While we liked the house we were renting, it bordered a very busy gas station. Tanker trucks made gasoline deliveries about three times a week. Each time, the fumes came into our house. We knew regular exposure to the fumes was probably adding to our already overtaxed immune systems, so we began to talk about moving. We thought about buying a house, but we only qualified to borrow enough to build either a very elaborate dog house or a small shed. We asked God to show us what we should do.

One evening Eric and I were sitting in the living room discussing our need to move. Suddenly, a face appeared at our front-door window, startling us. We were surprised to see one of our good friends. He told us that he and his wife were concerned about our health issues and wanted us to be able to move. He acknowledged the difficulty we were running into in our search. Then he said they wanted us to find a house that would be good for our allergies, and they would buy it. We could rent it from them for the cost of the mortgage payment. When we were able, we could buy it from them, and all our rent money would go toward the purchase price. They weren't going to charge us interest either.

As he spoke, we felt as if we were dreaming. Most people don't experience someone showing up at their door unannounced to make such an overwhelmingly generous offer.

We were humbled by their love and concern and by their willingness to sacrifice for our family. We knew God was using them to show His love for us.

We found a house at the entrance of a cul-de-sac and moved in the day before Daniel's first birthday. The layout of the house was great for my CFS, because there were only short flights of steps instead of a long staircase. We settled in and thoroughly enjoyed becoming part of our new neighborhood. It's a close neighborhood where neighbors borrow eggs or milk and share hand-me-down clothes.

An added bonus for us was the fact that the previous owners attended our church. They left behind a couch, all the window treatments, a lawn mower, the refrigerator and stove, a chest freezer, and an assortment of useful items. The Lord richly blessed us with our home!

Once we moved in, life finally settled into a routine. Although we weren't in full-time ministry as we hoped to be, it felt so good to be in our own home with the ability to plant our roots once again. We didn't feel so lost and without direction. Despite the trials we had been through, we were able to see God's hand on our family, and we were grateful for His presence and guidance.

Although we didn't understand why He had allowed the trials, our omniscient Father knew why they were necessary. He knew that we needed to keep a childlike grip on His hand.

Chapter 13

Losing Hope

THE YEAR 1998 began with the exciting news that we were going to have another baby. We looked forward to the enjoyable months of getting ready for our third child.

The happy atmosphere that news sparked in our family was in stark contrast with what was soon to follow. We were blissfully unaware that we were heading into the worst storms we had ever faced. It was a good thing the Lord had previously used some dark-colored threads in our tapestry.

The first dark clouds that appeared had been far out on the horizon for many years, although not in as dark a shade as they were now. My parents' marriage was struggling. In retrospect, as I said in an earlier chapter, I believe my Dad was bipolar. While he always came across as outgoing, happy, and jovial, a different side of him was locked away inside. He struggled with a destructive simmering depression and a very low self-esteem.

Mom was the only person regularly exposed to the depths of Dad's depression. He alternated between leaning heavily on her emotionally and resenting the help she tried to give him. They spent a considerable sum of money seeing counselors over the years, but none helped them in a lasting way. I believe the reason for that is because they both had chemical imbalances that needed medical intervention. Had they received proper treatment along with counseling, I believe the tragic events that unfolded would not have taken place.

We had seen the tension rising between them over the years beginning when I went to college. Seeing them not getting along so often was painful enough, but when the subject of separation arose, I couldn't believe it was happening to our family. My parents had always been admired for their close relationship and great teamwork. They both knew and loved the Lord.

In the midst of trying to deal with that situation, I had difficulties with my pregnancy at nineteen weeks. On April 20, I began having pain in my abdomen. Lin came to stay with Benjamin and Daniel, and Eric took me to the hospital.

An exterior monitor showed I was in pre-term labor. My doctor ordered a medication that eventually calmed down the contractions. I was discharged in the morning with instructions to be at the doctor's office in an hour and a half. We went home for a short rest. Lin met us at the door, exhausted after her fitful night of waiting and praying.

After his examination, the doctor ordered complete bed-rest. He gave me a prescription for a medication to hinder the contractions and arranged for me to see a specialist in high-risk pregnancies.

The day after the pre-term labor began, Dad called to tell me he had left Mom because they needed a time of separation. I couldn't imagine what they must have been feeling, but I was very aware of the pain the news created in me.

Shortly after I went on bed-rest, Eric's best friend, Jeff Wood, and another one of our good friends, Gregg Terry, stopped by unannounced to pray with us. They knelt at the foot of the mattress and prayed for God to protect our baby's life.

For me, it was a sacred experience in which our unborn child was irrevocably given to God for the protection only He could give. It became a defining moment and a solid benchmark to look back upon in the days ahead.

Eric moved our bed into the family room and placed a card table next to it, so I had easy access to necessary items. It helped to be a short distance from our half bath, because any movement caused contractions. I dubbed our new bedroom the Hilton Honeymoon Suite.

Even though I took medicine around the clock every four hours for three doses, then one dose at six hours and back to four again, I had contractions every day. The longest period of time I went without them during the four and a half months I remained on bed-rest was two days in a row.

I was relieved when Dad moved back in with Mom. However, despite more counseling, seeking help at a Christian facility, and going to a marriage retreat, their relationship continued to be marked by conflict. It was so troubling to me that I told them I could no longer listen to either of them talk about the other, because I needed to protect our baby from the turmoil I was experiencing over their situation.

Eric and the boys and I were trying to adjust to me being in bed. Even with all the extra work that Eric and Benjamin, who had just turned thirteen, did, they couldn't keep up with everything. Once again, our West Side family stepped in to help us. They provided rides to appointments, meals, childcare, help with housework, encouraging notes and calls, and solid prayer support.

Our insurance company's case manager for high-risk pregnancies arranged for visiting nurses to come three times a week to check on the baby and me. When I needed lab work, a technician came to the house.

As the days went by, I watched in awe as God provided help for our family.

One day, Dad called to say he had moved out again. I was having a hard time accepting the reality of what was happening between my parents. I couldn't imagine them living apart, nor did I want to. I yearned for the situation to improve and was full of fear and anguish about it. I needed them, and I needed them together.

Before I went on bed-rest, we had purchased tickets to go to an amusement park in June. My dad agreed to come up to help Eric with the boys. I dreaded the pain of having one of my parents visit without the other, even though I was eager to see Dad.

I tried to prepare myself. My family wasn't going to be home when he arrived, so I would have to face it by myself. I wasn't ready for the unwanted change to be so blatantly obvious. Dad wasn't even in sight when I observed the first difference. I heard his truck pull in the driveway and realized I was used to hearing their car instead.

Dad came across the porch and stopped in front of the window. Pressing his nose against the glass, he gave me a funny look and then came in the door. My heart sank when he came in by himself. I wanted Mom to be with him. I wondered what holidays and birthdays would be like if their separation became permanent. How would we celebrate the special events and milestones of life that are such a big part of belonging to a family? Those thoughts flew through my mind before Dad reached my bedside and bent over to give me a hug and kiss. As he had done so many times in the past, he gave me a red rosebud, and then left the room to get a vase.

When he was out of sight, I stared at the beautiful flower. Of course, it would be a rose. Dad called me "Rosebud." Mom was also involved in the use of that name. I could still see her holding out the cake pan on my twelfth birthday, as she, Dad, and Jimmy surprised me before I was out of bed. Mom had decorated the cake with numerous rosebuds. The memory brought an intense longing for Mom's presence.

As I heard Dad coming back, I struggled to retain control of my emotions. He set the vase next to the bed and went out to unload his truck. A painful lump in my throat made it hard to swallow. Hot tears welled up in my eyes, threatening to spill over. I feared I would lose my composure entirely.

When he came back in, he had a red-and-black clothes-carrier bag slung across his shoulder and a medium-size cardboard box under his arm. He said that Mom sent up some items for us. She had set them out on the back porch for him to pick up before he left. My heart wrenched at the thought of such an arrangement.

Mom sent four boxes of baby girl clothes she picked up at yard sales for us, now that we knew we were having a girl. The clothes-carrier bag was for us as well. I felt as if I were dreaming. It couldn't really be happening! But it was. Dad finished unloading the truck and offered to show me the clothes Mom sent.

The irony of him being there without her, showing me the clothes she had gotten for us, served to drive the painful reality of their separation deeper in my heart.

Dad lifted each washed and folded item, turned it to show me both sides, and then set it in a pile. The meticulous care with which the garments had been packed was a silent witness to my mother's love and care. It was inconceivable to me that she couldn't be there.

When the nurse arrived for her visit, I was eager for Dad to hear the baby's heartbeat. We had chosen the name Naomi Elizabeth, and Dad and Mom both faithfully prayed for her by name each day. Dad's eyes were bright with anticipation; they really lit up at the rhythm of the rapid heartbeat. Naomi moved, and a beaming smile crossed Dad's face when he felt her strong kicks bumping up against his palm. I could picture him holding Naomi, just as he had held her brothers before her.

The morning of the amusement park trip dawned bright and promised to be a picture-perfect day. Dad was going to leave the park earlier than Eric and was going to check on me before he went home.

After they left, silence settled over the house, and sadness flooded my heart. I enjoyed getting to see Dad; yet, I missed Mom so much, and his presence without her served as a continual reminder of her absence.

I was concerned for both of them and thought about my recent interactions with Dad. He had said he felt himself beginning to unwind inside, but he missed Mom so much that he could hardly stand it. He didn't want Mom to know how much he missed her, because he didn't want to give her false hope that they would get back together. He broke down and sobbed when he told me he had given up hope that their relationship would ever improve.

I had heard my dad cry only a couple of times in my life. Hearing him cry and say he had lost all hope scared me just as much as it made me sad. From the depression I had experienced, I knew firsthand about losing hope and the distorted thinking it causes.

I grew fearful that Dad would commit suicide and repeatedly urged him to get help. He always refused, saying that all the years of counseling they had received had not accomplished anything, and he didn't want to waste more money. I told him he needed to seek help specifically for his depression. He said he wasn't in a depression, a pronouncement he made while crying. I told him he didn't know enough about depression to know that he was in one and that I was concerned he would get to the point where he would see suicide as his only way out of the pain. I expressed my fear about him committing suicide and questioned him about it in multiple conversations. Every time he told me he would never do that to us. He always assured me that I didn't ever need to worry about him committing suicide.

The day went by quickly as I waited for Dad to get back from the park. I set aside my school books when I heard his truck pull in the driveway. He came in and visited for a bit. I could tell from the sparkle in his eyes that he had enjoyed the time with Eric and the boys. It was wonderful to see him so happy. For a moment, my heart wasn't as heavy.

All of a sudden, he looked at his watch and said he had to leave. He was going to stop at his friends' hunting cabin to mow the lawn and spruce up the place before they arrived there that evening.

He gave me a hug and kiss, then patted my abdomen, pausing a moment to see if he could feel Naomi move.

He said a final good-bye and walked out of the room. I watched him go across the front porch, aware that his departure was in stark contrast with his arrival. Instead of stopping to make another funny face, he didn't even look my way as he passed the window with a resolute stride. I heard the familiar sound of his keys jingling, as he shook them in his pocket.

Later that evening, I called to make sure he had made it back safely. At first, when he didn't answer, I wasn't too concerned. As the evening progressed, I began to be afraid he had been in an accident. I continued to call his number every few minutes.

When he finally answered the phone around 11:30, hot tears were dripping off my chin, and I could barely choke out the question, "Where have you been?" He said he had been stuck at the caretaker's cottage until a bad electrical storm passed. He had just returned. He apologized for causing me so much concern. I told him that I had been afraid he had been in an accident, and that I couldn't take it if anything happened to him. I told him how much he meant to me and how much I needed him. When I finally calmed down and hung up, I was utterly drained.

I continued to have regular contact with Dad. Each time, I listened for clues about what was going on inside him. Sometimes I felt reassured about his emotional state; other times a nagging fear remained when we got off the phone.

When he called one night the week after he had been to see us, I was very troubled by his demeanor. He had a hopeless view of not only his marriage but of his future. He didn't know what he was going to do and couldn't come up with any options. Financially he was strapped. He didn't think he could continue to paint forever, because it was wearing out some of his joints. His retirement package wasn't going to help much.

All my life, my dad had been a figure of strength. He had been the one whom people counted on to fix their problems. To hear him sound so helpless and hopeless sent fear through me.

I suggested he develop a larger clientele and hire painters to work for him. He could line up jobs and live off a percentage of the revenue.

His immediate response wasn't what I expected, but it reflected his emotional disarray. He said he couldn't do it because he wouldn't know how to organize something like that. My dad saying he couldn't organize something made no sense to me. He had been organizing things my entire life like the yearly Hunter's Safety program, intramural basketball, all-school activity days, the swimming program at the Benton Dam, faculty get-togethers, and the yearly appreciation breakfast for the cafeteria staff.

I pointed out the fact that he had a reputation as a painter with a solid work ethic and a penchant for detailed perfection. He already had a wonderful foundation for what could become a good business. I told him I knew he could do it.

He sounded overwhelmed and mumbled that he wouldn't even know where to start. I gave him several ideas, but he claimed he didn't have that kind of ability.

I was getting my first glimpse at the inner world of self-doubt and conflict in Dad's heart. He had no confidence in his ability to come up with a plan, let alone carry it out. The essential element of hope was draining out of him at a rapidly increasing rate.

Hearing his desperately hopeless outlook resurrected my fear about the possibility of him committing suicide. I brought up the subject again. I asked him outright if he was thinking of suicide, and once again warned him of the danger of getting to the point where suicide looked like his only way out of the pain. He again told me that he absolutely never would do that to me—or to any of us—and I didn't need to worry about him ever committing suicide. He said it simply wasn't an option for him. He then ended by saying something he had never said before. He said, "You don't have to worry about it, and I would appreciate it if you quit asking me about it." His tone wasn't angry, but it was said in such a way that it made a point. With those words it was as though he put his hand up as a policeman would when stopping traffic.

He was essentially telling me to back off, without saying it in so many words. He had drawn a line in the sand and had set the boundary he wanted me to live within.

His statement caused me grave concern. *Why did he tell me to back off? Is he truly not considering it and is just stressed out by my bringing it up so often? Is he pushing me away because I'm getting too close to a truth he doesn't want me to discover?*

I didn't know what to do. I thought about calling one of Dad's good friends and disclosing my fear that he might be considering suicide. However, when I thought about someone confronting him about it, I was afraid he would be angry with me for talking with someone. I also feared that if he was considering it, a confrontation might be the catalyst for him to go through with it quickly. In the end, my desire to avoid making Dad angry prevailed, and I decided to wait longer before contacting his friends.

Over the next two weeks we continued to talk regularly. While I was still concerned about him, I also began to see some positive signs of progress in his outlook. He was active and talked about plans for the week.

On July 4, he had a cookout with a couple at the cabin. That evening he seemed happy with how the day had gone.

He also accepted an invitation to a party hosted by one of the high school teachers. Realizing it would have been awkward for him to anticipate the probability of having to discuss his failing marriage, I was encouraged by what he had done. I thought it represented a big step in the right direction. He wasn't being reclusive.

I was beginning to relax more about him as he continued to stay busy and talk about future events.

A couple of days later, I had a pleasant surprise. Two of Dad's sisters came from Pennsylvania to visit for a few hours. I was so happy to see them. Dad had given them directions to our house and kept it a secret so they could surprise me.

We had a wonderful visit, and I felt better after they left. My spirits had been lifted, and I was able to refocus on the anticipation of Naomi's birth.

Chapter 14

Grieving a Suicide

THAT EVENING, I told Dad about my surprise visitors. He was glad they found our house without any problems and had taken the time to come. He talked about plans for the week, including getting the grip replaced on his golf clubs. He was looking forward to golfing with Jimmy on Saturday. It was great to hear him sound so good.

The following night Dad said he hated to cut our time short, but he needed to finish putting up his new mailbox. He was running out of daylight and wanted to have it done by dark. Even though I wanted him to be home with Mom, I was glad he was taking another step in facing life. I was encouraged by each sign of emotional improvement.

Our conversation the next evening was much longer. I told him about my OB/GYN appointment that day, and he asked a lot of questions about Naomi's development. He wanted to know if we had reached the point where she would survive if she were born. I told him we couldn't know for sure, because a lot of it would depend on her lung development. Then he asked, "Does the doctor think she will make it if she were born now?"

I said, "He can't be sure, but he said he feels she would have a better chance of making it than not making it. She might have to be in the hospital for a long time, but she would probably survive."

Dad sighed deeply and said, "That's very good news."

Since we all had been eager to get to the point in the pregnancy when we could breathe a little easier, I didn't think much about Dad's persistent questioning.

We talked about other events of the day, and then Dad abruptly switched topics and began to talk about how much he loved me. He said he had always been proud of me from the moment I was born, and that I had brought him so much joy over the years. He expressed his love for my husband and children as well, but he mostly focused on how much he loved me and how much I meant to him.

What he said was everything a daughter could ever hope to hear from her father. As he continued to affirm me, I almost said, "Dad, you sound like you expect to never talk to me again." Instead of interrupting, I just listened. I thought he was making sure I knew he would always love me no matter what happened between him and Mom. When he finished, I assured him that my deep love for him never would change.

The next day, Thursday, July 9, 1998, we received a phone call that changed my life. Eric was out of sight when he answered the phone in the kitchen. I heard him move into the dining room farther away from me. I couldn't make out what he was saying, but could tell he was mostly listening. I quit trying to strain my ears to hear some snatch of conversation and turned my attention back to my dessert. Blueberry pie always made me think of Dad because he loved it as much as I did.

I heard Eric hang up the phone and come toward me, so I lifted my head to meet his eyes. When I saw the look on his face, I immediately froze inside and steeled myself for what I knew was going to be bad news. Eric's ashen face was stricken with anguish. As he came down the stairs, I said urgently, "What? What is it, Eric? What happened?" Intuitively I knew it had to do with my parents. Were they getting a divorce? No, from Eric's face something far worse had happened. I guessed that one of my parents had been in a car accident and was either dead or wasn't expected to make it.

Eric crossed the distance between us, knelt down next to me, and took my hand in his. His red eyes were moist as he looked at me and said, "Maureen, your father committed suicide this afternoon."

Instantly, a hot, searing, invisible knife cut through my chest. Pain unlike anything I had ever experienced engulfed me. The reality of the horrendous finality of his action and the irreversible separation that now existed between us mercilessly branded my heart and left behind a raw wound. I began to scream and arose in a futile effort to get away from what I had just been told. As I got to my feet and felt a strong urge to wildly throw myself around, I thought of Naomi and realized I had to protect her. I sat back down and continued to scream, "No! No! Not my dad!"

Despite my previous concerns that Dad would commit suicide, I wasn't prepared to hear it had happened. I was taken so off guard; it was as though the possibility had never entered my mind. I couldn't believe that my dad, to whom I was so close, was dead by his own hand at the age of fifty-six.

I kept picturing a huge ship wheel in the room. The wheel represented time, and I envisioned myself trying to force it back the other way. I wanted to be able to move the clock back enough to get to the point where Dad was still alive, so I could stop him.

The Cassaras and Lohmans quickly arrived. I was deeply grateful for the presence of our best friends as we faced the darkest threads ever woven into our tapestry. They shared our sorrow and wept with us, and in so doing began to introduce some lighter colors into the fabric. God reached out to us in love through them.

They left around 11:30 that evening. Eric fell into an exhausted sleep, but I stayed awake the entire night. In the still darkness, I found myself acutely aware that I was alone with God. Only this time we were on previously untrodden ground. Crisis situations shake us up to the very foundations. I remember thinking, *This is where the rubber meets the road. How does this fit into my relationship with God, my thoughts about God, my view of God?*

I was struck by the sheer irony of the fact that God had all the necessary power to have prevented Dad's death, but He had chosen not to. He had allowed this painful event to take place. Yet, He was also the very same One I now turned to for comfort.

I felt awkward. It was as though I was anticipating meeting with a best friend who had acted in an unexpected way, resulting in my trying to regain my normal, comfortable familiarity and sense of being completely at ease with him. I didn't know how to act or what to say. I knew God hadn't changed, but I didn't know how to factor what had just taken place into our relationship.

It's easier to believe in a loving God when life is going smoothly than it is when facing a painful trial. The reality of Dad's suicide and the knowledge that God could have prevented it caused me to ask myself, *Just exactly what do I really believe? Maybe there really isn't a God.*

As soon as the thought crossed my mind, I rejected it. The intelligent design in God's creative handiwork loudly proclaims His existence. In addition, I had already experienced twenty-two years of personal relationship with Him. Allowing the tragedy to cause me to walk away from my belief in God and in His Word wasn't an option.

As I began to sort through the emotional fallout, I realized I needed to fill my mind with the truths of God's Word. I knew Satan wanted to work me over, whisper his lies, and try to get me to doubt God—His faithfulness, His power, and His love. I knew I had a choice to make. I was either going to continue to believe the truth about Him as revealed in His Word, or I would buy into Satan's lies and abandon truth.

In His goodness, God used my experience in Grenada to prepare me to realize the importance of clinging to Him instead of distancing myself from Him. I wanted to stay close to Him and not allow the pain to come between us. I don't know how I would have handled Dad's suicide if I hadn't had that experience. I do know that God used the lessons I learned from my spiritual and emotional struggles during that time for good in the wake of Dad's death. The foundational truths about His character and His Word were the pillars that remained standing when my world fell apart.

In the weeks leading up to Dad's death, the Lord had kept bringing Psalm 55:22 to my attention. It says, "Cast your cares on the LORD and he will sustain you; he will never let the righteous fall."

I wondered why God was showing it to me. I evaluated every area of my life I could think of to see if there was something I wasn't trusting God with. I couldn't think of anything, so I finally concluded that I just didn't know why He was showing me the verse.

Then the night that Dad died, God brought that verse to my mind. Instantly I knew that Dad's death was the reason He kept showing it to me. I told Him, "This is what it was all about. You knew he was going to do that, and You were preparing me for it."

What a comfort it was to know He knew, He had gone ahead to begin to prepare me for it, and He cared. The evidence of God's loving concern was a light-colored strand He wove into the tapestry during the dark hours after Dad's suicide.

Another way God ministered to me that night came in the form of a picture in my mind. The picture was of a figure, robed in white, head bowed, hands clasped together in front of him, with a saddened countenance, standing to the right of the fireplace. Now, before you close this book and never pick it up again—no, I didn't see God. I know it was just in my head, but I also know God put it there as His way of letting me know that He was with me, He shared my sorrow, and He was sad for me.

At first I found it comforting, but after a while I became frustrated. I said, *What are You doing just standing there? Do something! You're the God of this universe and You have all power to do whatever You want to do. I want You to raise my dad from the dead. I need my dad. You can raise him for me, just like You raised Lazarus. That's what I want You to do.*

Even as I spoke, I knew He wasn't going to bring Dad back from the dead for me. As the hours passed, the fact of His presence became a comfort to me again, and I began to be very grateful for the blessing of His companionship.

Sure, I would much rather He had miraculously intervened with another Lazarus scene in a tremendous display of His awesome power; but I knew it wasn't going to happen that way.

It's easy to miss the most important aspect of God's involvement in heartbreaking situations. Sometimes we focus so much energy on wondering what God will do in answer to our prayers that we fail to recognize and appreciate the gift He does give us—the gift of His presence.

If we're not careful, we can become like those in the crowd who followed Jesus merely to see a demonstration of His power but left His side once the miracle was done. We all like it when there is bread to eat and baskets of leftovers. What happens when we're still hungry and there isn't anything to eat?

One other important interaction between the Lord and me took place that night. I hurt so much inside that I felt as if my heart was totally broken. I envisioned it not just shattered into pieces but totally crushed and reduced to nothing but dust. I wondered what God was going to do to "bind up the brokenhearted" as the Scripture refers to in Isaiah 61:1. I told the Lord, *But there's nothing left but dust for You to work with. There aren't even whole pieces anymore.*

Immediately, and unmistakably, He responded in my mind, "I made Adam out of the dust of the ground, and I created the world out of nothing. I can put your heart back together."

As the night wore on, I struggled to make sense of what was taking place. I was experiencing such intense pain while the Great Physician stood by, withholding His power to make it better. I tried to reconcile the irony of being alone with the One who chose not to stop it from happening, yet was deeply distressed Himself.

Then I was reminded that God had already prevented it from happening at least one other time. Five days after my wedding, Dad was going to commit suicide. He had everything in place and was going to call his friend and ask him to come to the house on a pretense of needing help with something. Dad wanted to have his friend find him instead of Mom finding him when she arrived home. Thankfully, when he tried to call his friend, the phone line was dead for no human reason. Without that part of his plan in place, Dad decided not to go through with it. *Thank you, Lord! You gave us fourteen more years with Dad.*

Although God stopped him in June 1984, He didn't intervene on July 9, 1998. I've often wondered what lengths God went to in the days before Dad's death to try to talk him out of it. I'm sure He was deeply grieved with each step Dad took in putting his plan into motion.

When the first light began to filter into the room the morning after Dad died, I was glad the long night was coming to an end. I wished the events of the previous day had been only a dream, but the intense rawness of my emotions was a continual reminder of the living nightmare that had just begun.

Often, in the realm of Christianity, there's a strong unspoken desire to see perfectly placid people calmly accept whatever tragedy comes their way; or to see God miraculously pluck them from their problem.

It's as though any expression of negative emotions is a sure sign that something is wrong with the system, and we don't want there to be anything wrong with it. We don't want to experience pain. We want Jesus to make everything better and not allow us to suffer.

Some people grow uncomfortable when others openly express their suffering. They want to take out a "holy bandage," slap it on the wound, and have instant healing take place—and without an allergic reaction to the latex in the bandage!

When you think of God helping a person who is suffering or in need, what do you think of Him doing to help in the situation? Do you think He will show up with an impressive display of His omnipotence? Maybe so, but more often than not, He quietly shows up unannounced and unrecognized.

In times of pain we need to be careful, or we might not realize what God is doing to help us. One thing we can know for sure: He is on the scene working on our behalf. The problem is, we often look for Him in all the wrong places.

In 1 Kings, God used the prophet Elijah to reveal His power in a showdown with the prophets of Baal on top of Mount Carmel (18:20). It culminated in a spectacular display of God's power when the fire of the Lord fell and burned up the sacrifice, the wood, the stones, and the soil, and also licked up all the water in the trench around the altar (18:38). Following that, the prophets of Baal were killed (18:40). Jezebel, the king's wife, wasn't too happy with the news, so she threatened to kill Elijah. He left town as fast as his feet could carry him (19:2–3). In fear, he fled to the desert, where he collapsed in a heap, utterly drained. He sat under a broom tree and prayed that he would die (19:4). It didn't make sense for him to run away to protect his life, only to sit down and pray for his death!

Some people criticize Elijah for his response to Jezebel's threat. They wonder how, after he witnessed all that amazing stuff on Mount Carmel, he could run for his life because a woman threatened him. Not only that, but she threatened him based on the very gods that had just been proven to be false!

What happened? Elijah was in the valley after the mountaintop victory in heavy-duty spiritual warfare. There's a very real energy that's depleted when we're involved in spiritual warfare.

On top of that, in the power of the Lord, Elijah had run a great distance at a pace that beat King Ahab's chariot back to the city of Jezreel (18:46). He was completely exhausted—spiritually, physically, mentally, and emotionally.

Before I go any further, I have a couple of questions. How would you have handled Elijah? How do you handle people you come across who are in a similarly depleted condition? Some advocate a "pick yourself up by the bootstraps and get going" approach. Let's see what God did.

God understood Elijah's needs, and He addressed them in a practical way. His first order of business was to allow Elijah to lie down and get some needed sleep (19:5). Then He had an angel wake him up to eat and drink what was divinely prepared for him, after which he lay down for more sleep (19:6). The angel came back a second time and told him to eat because the journey was too much for him (19:7). Elijah ate and drank and was strengthened by that food. He traveled forty days and nights until he reached Mount Horeb, where he went into a cave and spent the night (19:7–9).

Elijah was then told to go out and stand on the mountain in the presence of the Lord, because the Lord was about to pass by (19:11). First, a powerful wind tore the mountains apart and shattered the rocks. After that, an earthquake occurred. The earthquake was followed by a fire (19:11–12).

Most of us would probably expect God to have been in the wind, earthquake, or the fire. After all, they're dramatic displays of power, and God is indeed powerful. However, the Bible says that God wasn't in any of them (19:11–12). If Elijah was looking for God in them, he was looking in the wrong places—just as we do sometimes.

On top of the mountain that day, God chose to reveal Himself to Elijah in a still, small voice—a gentle whisper. In the ensuing conversation, God dealt with Elijah's fears and misconceptions, and He gave him his next assignment (19:12–18).

I love that story because it shows my awesome God in action. He didn't berate Elijah or write him off as a loser. Instead, He met Elijah where he was and ministered to him in the small ways that addressed Elijah's very tangible needs.

When Elijah was tired, he didn't find a comfortable mattress in the desert to curl up on, but he did get the sleep he needed. When he was hungry, he didn't come across a newly opened convenience store in the middle of nowhere, but he did get to eat a cake of bread baked over hot coals. When he was thirsty, he didn't find the mother spring of bottled water, but he did get to drink from a jar of water God provided.

We err when we look for God to work only in big, spectacular, miraculous ways. However, when we open our eyes and see what is truly around us, we will recognize His hand at work in many, often small, ways. Whether small or large, quiet or loud, natural or supernatural, methods do not limit the hand of God when ministering to His children in need. Just don't miss seeing His hand in the small things.

Chapter 15

Adjusting to the Void

IN THE DAYS after Dad's death, I saw God's hand of blessing, love, and care. He used many small acts of kindness and ministry to introduce light-colored threads into the tapestry.

Dad's viewing was scheduled for Sunday night; his funeral would be Monday. I couldn't make the trip, but I wanted to have a part in the service. Eric said he would read something for me, so I started writing a tribute.

The day after Dad's death a visiting nurse came. Ironically, it was the same nurse who had met him. She was shocked at the news, and it stirred up painful memories for her. Years before, her best friend had committed suicide. She still felt betrayed.

I was amazed that the Lord provided a nurse who could identify with what we were going through. It was another way God reached out to me in my pain.

The following day, the weekend nurse told me her brother had made repeated attempts to commit suicide, and she still had concerns about him. Those conversations were the beginning of my learning how common suicide is in our society.

The doctor had warned me that dehydration could bring on labor, so I tried to remember to keep drinking water throughout the day. I wanted to protect Naomi, and I didn't want to allow the situation to cause me to forget.

As news of Dad's death traveled, friends and neighbors came with words of condolence, flowers, cards, and food. In between visitors, I continued to write.

The day was a marathon race against the clock. By evening I was exhausted from the draining emotions, the intense writing pace, and lack of sleep. When I got ready for bed, I didn't know if my body would relax after the adrenalin overdrive of the day. Thankfully, it did; and for the first time since I had gotten the news, I slept.

The next morning I finished my tribute in time for Eric to read through it once before he left for the funeral. Ladies from church were going to stay with me while he was away.

About two hours after he left, I started having contractions. My abdomen distended as Naomi curled into a tight ball. With a sinking heart, I realized I had gotten distracted and had neglected to drink enough water.

The Lord provided a visiting nurse at the perfect time. She called the doctor, and he told me to go to the hospital.

Lin Lohman took me to the third floor triage unit. They quickly hooked me up to a machine to monitor the contractions. A nurse tried to start an intravenous line to rehydrate me, but was unsuccessful. A second nurse had the same result. They brought in a third nurse, known for her ability to succeed in hard cases. She lived up to her reputation, and they started giving me fluids.

To my left, I had a clear view of the wall clock. Throughout the evening, I looked at it periodically, and watched its hands make their circular orbit. As the time for the viewing approached, I wanted to silence the methodical ticking in an effort to stop time and change what was taking place at McMichael's Funeral Home in Benton.

Lin stayed with me. I was thankful for her presence. She managed to get a phone for me to use. I called the funeral home and spoke with my uncle. It was comforting to hear his voice and to have contact with family during the service. Hours later, I talked with him again. He said the last people were making their way through the line. It was two hours after the viewing was supposed to have ended.

As the fluids accomplished their purpose, the contractions slowed down and I began to feel better. When the doctor was sure Naomi and I were stable, Lin took me home.

The following morning, Lin and her family went on vacation. Before she left, she brought over a decorative bag with items to remind me that she would be thinking of me and praying for me.

Carol Cassara and another friend from church, Linda Cribbs, were staying with me. After breakfast they asked if there was anything special I'd like to do to mark the day of Dad's funeral. I appreciated their thoughtfulness and consideration.

For some reason, it was important to me to take a shower and be clean in time for his service. The Lord graciously allowed my first shower in months to go smoothly. Afterward, I felt I was ready for the service I wouldn't attend. We had our own service with Scripture and prayer.

Before he took his life, Dad wrote individual notes to some family members and friends. He gave them to his landlady and asked her to deliver them for him. When she realized what he was about to do, she tried to talk him out of it. Although his red eyes betrayed the depths of his conflicting emotional upheaval, he told her it was too late for him to get the type of help he needed. With that, he drove a short distance down the road, entered the woods, and robbed himself—and us—of the gift of his life.

His landlady called the state police immediately, but Dad left no time for intervention once he set his plan in motion. When the police arrived, they confiscated the notes he had written. They were material evidence in the investigation. We had to wait several frustrating weeks before police protocol allowed us to obtain the notes and read his final words to us.

After the police released Dad's notes, Eric and I received the ones for us. I looked at Dad's familiar handwriting on the envelope addressed to me, and I ached to be with him. I was keenly aware that my last communication with him was contained in the words on the piece of paper in my hand. Part of me wanted to read it quickly so I could know what he had said to me. Another part of me was very conscious of the finality that reading it would bring. This would be it. There wouldn't be any more messages from him. It was his last communication with me, and my last contact on earth with him.

I opened the letter. The note was reflective of the loving relationship we had shared. He thanked God that because of Jesus, our separation would be temporary, and he told me he would see me in heaven. He thanked me for the wonderful son-in-law and grandchildren I had given him, and he assured me of his unending love for me. His words soothed my heart as I felt the love with which he had written them.

In contrast, his postscript was frustrating. In it, he said he hadn't been lying to me when he told me that ending it all was not an option. It had just become so painful for him that it had become his only way out of the pain.

I said aloud, "I warned you, Dad. I told you that was exactly what could happen." If only he had listened to me!

In the weeks following Dad's death, I put some of my thoughts on paper in the following poem, which I then turned into a song.

Refrain:
Why did you have to die that day?
It didn't have to be that way
You could have gone for help for your problems
Your pain could have gone away
And then you'd still be here today

Verses:
As your pain grew greater
You stuffed it all inside.
Depression told you lies
And you thought of suicide.
Oh, you should have called someone for help
You should have picked up the phone.
Instead you chose to use your gun
And you left us all alone.

The irony of your last act
Is that your pain lives on.
You thought you ended it that day
And yet it isn't gone.
Instead, you placed on all of us
What you said you could not bear.
Now our hearts hold the pain you had.
Oh, Dad, it's just not fair.

Each day we go on living
We have to face the fact
Your life on earth is over
We cannot bring you back.
Someday we'll see you once again
With Jesus we'll all be.
Thank God, the saved will live together
Throughout eternity.

The hole you left behind you
Is deep and very wide.
Nothing will ever fill the gap
You left the day you died.
We miss you, oh so very much
And we wish you could have seen
The consequences of your act
And what it would all mean.

Adjusting to the death of a loved one is a painful experience. Adjusting to a death by suicide adds a unique, intensely complicated dimension to the process.

In some cases, the horrific violence of the act defies contemplation, yet rudely and persistently demands consideration.

The knowledge that it didn't need to happen leaves survivors without a comprehensible cause and effect to aid their acceptance. There is no disease, bacteria, virus, illness, drunk driver, failed brakes, icy road, flash flood, dangerous occupation, hideous assailant, or any other tangible factor to cling to that provides an understandable, albeit regrettable, reason for the death. Instead, the will of the deceased is the sole cause, an explanation that is pregnant with questions but barren of answers.

The suddenness of the loss spawns within the survivor an unreasonable—and at times overwhelming—fear of experiencing another sudden loss.

The premature nature of the death prevents the survivor from having the opportunity to say good-bye to the victim. In cases where notes are left, the victim has taken the opportunity to say what he or she wanted to say. The survivor is never given the chance to respond. Instead, he or she must live with an unfinished, one-sided final conversation.

Our family faced the formidable task of adjusting to the void in our lives caused by Dad's death. The anticipated beginning of our daughter's life outside the womb was in stark contrast to the resounding finality of Dad's death. These two factors formed the backdrop for the rest of my time on bed-rest.

A couple of months after Dad's death, I did some reading about bipolar disorder and felt it was the undiagnosed cause of his chemical imbalance. Soon after, a medical professional initiated the subject with me and voiced the same opinion, not knowing of my thoughts on the matter. I became convinced that Dad's problem had been identified. I regretted it was two months too late.

In His goodness, the Lord kept Naomi safe and growing in the womb until two weeks before her delivery date. Our red headed daughter was born in the early fall of 1998. We were so thankful to the Lord for protecting her life and for bringing us through the four and a half months of bed-rest.

It took until the middle of November for me to have the necessary strength to make the trip to Pennsylvania. Even though I knew Dad was gone, I had an unreasonable, persistent feeling that if I searched long and hard enough there, I'd be able to find him and make everything okay again.

As we pulled up the driveway, my eyes swept the property, searching for the one I knew wouldn't be there. It was exactly the same, yet entirely different. Surely Dad would emerge from the pole barn any moment. I could even picture how he would be dressed. He would have on a white tee shirt tucked into his stained white painter's pants, and he would be wearing his brown painting shoes.

We got out of the car and heard the familiar sound of the back screen door slamming shut. In an exceptional display of courage and love, Mom faced us alone and cheerfully called out her normal greeting as she came toward us on the sidewalk. I was grateful for her attempt to meet us with the same level of enthusiasm and tradition as before. I marveled at her ability to find the necessary inner fortitude to give us such a welcome.

I could only imagine her emotions as she watched the clock and waited for us to arrive. I could picture her praying and fighting for control of her tears when she heard the crunch of our tires coming up the long driveway. Her ability to think of us and project a positive outlook was beyond my understanding. I tremendously appreciated her effort on our behalf. It served to set a tone of determination to continue on and not allow Dad's death to destroy the rest of our family.

During that first trip after his death, Eric and I went to the property where Dad had been staying. We talked with his landlady and then drove the short distance down the road to where Dad killed himself. The peaceful wooded setting betrayed no evidence of the violence it had witnessed.

We made one final visit. Eric had taken pictures of Dad's grave, but I wanted to see it for myself. He was buried in St. Gabriel's cemetery, a grassy, sloping field bordered by a mature, mixed forest of pines and deciduous trees. Ironically and fittingly, the Boy Scout camp property where he loved to spend time when he was a boy is on the other side of the road going past the quiet country cemetery.

Mom and I spent much of the week sorting through Dad's workshop in the pole barn. We also got rid of Dad's clothes. We took them to a church that was holding a clothing drive for an overseas destination. As we unloaded, I had an odd feeling that was hard to shake. I felt as if we were giving Dad away. I had emotionally tied my ability to feel close to him with the visual sight of his clothes. Disposing of his belongings was a necessary part of the process and one that Mom really needed my help with. Yet, as each box and bag was unloaded, I felt myself unwillingly pushed into facing in a fresh way, the harsh reality of his irreversible absence.

Actually, I was reminded of his absence by many aspects of daily living. When the phone rang, I expected it to be him. Our history course in homeschool that year covered material my dad had taught me in public school. He had taught both Eric and me during our seventh and tenth-grade years. I had looked forward to Dad telling Benjamin many of the same fascinating historical stories.

There was also the loss of his broad base of knowledge in a variety of areas such as painting, fishing, the outdoors, hunting, camping, teaching, and life skills. The inability to call him for answers or advice was a frustrating reminder of his absence. I was thankful I could still call Mom and tap into her wisdom and knowledge; however, she was in the same boat as I when it came to certain topics.

There was no getting around the fact that Dad was totally cut off from any involvement in my life, and I felt the loss keenly. I had a different view of future events. There were so many anticipated milestones he would have shared with us. Now, some events wouldn't take place. Others would still happen, but they wouldn't be the same without him. Birthdays, holidays, and other gatherings served as a reminder that he was gone.

There were many objects that didn't affect other people, but the sight of them set my emotions on an unbidden, wild roller-coaster ride. Rosebuds, Peppermint Patties, history books, my teacher's plan book, sports magazines, hunting or fishing equipment, boats, ponds, cross-country skies, wildlife, ball hats, board games, Ford pick-ups, ice cream, mushroom soup, salt and pepper, French fries, pizza, coffee, painting equipment, blueberry or apple pie, shaving cream, and carrots are some of the things that evoked a strong emotional response in me. Hearing certain songs was bittersweet. When I saw other grandparents enjoying their grandchildren or middle-aged couples holding hands, I'd think, *That should be you and Mom. You should still be here.*

In the year following Dad's death, I struggled a great deal with *why.* One day, a homeschool conference speaker named Jeff Myers said something that clicked in my heart. He said, "Sometimes we don't get our answers to life's questions—especially the *why* questions in this life. Some things just aren't going to be answered or totally understood in this life, and that is okay. In eternity it will all make sense."

I've found that, as one person put it, "Finding meaning in suffering isn't usually found by asking the question, 'Why did this happen?' Rather, as we see God use it for good, we find meaning in the midst of suffering."

I have also come to understand what Hudson Taylor meant when he wrote the following in a dark moment of his life: "It doesn't matter how great the pressure is. What really matters is where the pressure lies—whether it comes between you and God or whether it presses you nearer His heart."

Trials are opportunities for God to use His power to strengthen us spiritually. He wants us to be confident of His love for us and to continue to place our trust in Him. As He strengthens us from within, He enables us to withstand increased pressure from without. It is His strength, not ours, that can be relied upon (see Ephesians 3:16–21).

Dad's death was the worst trial I had faced in life. The Lord used the pressure to bring me closer to Him. He knew I would soon be facing another and would need to draw heavily from the lessons He had taught me and the spiritual strengthening He had accomplished in my heart.

Chapter 16

Spiraling Downward

WHENEVER A PERSON commits suicide, he or she leaves behind people who question themselves and wonder if they could have done something differently that would have affected the outcome. If only I had . . . . If I hadn't . . . . I should have . . . . How did I miss seeing . . . ? I should have followed through on . . . .

Those of us who have lost a loved one to suicide are emotionally vulnerable to experiencing false guilt. The truth is that suicide is a choice. It is one of the most selfish choices a person can make.

Suicide is a death sentence for those who kill themselves, and a life sentence for those left behind.

Everyone goes through painful experiences, but not everyone chooses to deal with pain the same way. Those who choose suicide are not forced into anything. They make a choice to end life.

In the wake of a suicide, those closest to the deceased are often afraid they contributed in some way to the person's death. They replay their interactions with the deceased, especially their last interaction, and second-guess themselves.

I realize that some of you might have experienced a negative interaction such as a heated argument as your last interaction with your friend or loved one. Maybe your loved one committed suicide immediately after a tense conflict with you. Maybe you said, "I don't care. Go ahead and do it!" to a person's threat to kill himself or herself. If you lost your loved one to suicide and you blame yourself for that death, please listen to me: Suicide is a choice. You are not to blame. Let go of the false guilt, or it will eat away at you like an emotional cancer.

You're not the only one who has felt the constricting emotions associated with being a survivor of suicide. Find a counselor who can help you deal with the trauma you've experienced. Pain doesn't just go away. If not dealt with properly, it might be pushed down inside and not felt as much, but it's still there and will affect you in negative ways. It's like an abscess that needs to be lanced so the infection can be cleaned out and the area can heal properly.

Dad's suicide plunged Mom into a world of tumultuous and sometimes paralyzing emotions. A fear of abandonment had been her companion since childhood. Now her fear had materialized and become reality, a reality that took on a life and voice of its own and pronounced her unfit to love. It didn't matter that the message wasn't true; all that mattered was that it was being spoken.

Mom was trapped in a vicious internal conflict as she tried to deal with Dad's decision to kill himself. On one level, she correctly knew she wasn't responsible for his death. Yet, her self-doubt and merciless introspection produced an accusation of personal responsibility.

The truth about their marriage conflicts is that Dad and Mom both had chemical imbalances that affected every aspect of their lives, including their marriage. Had they been properly diagnosed and received the necessary medical intervention, I believe their imbalances could have been corrected. Mom had been on and off medication for her chronic, recurring depression. Dad never knew he had a chemical imbalance. They had spent a considerable amount of time and money on counseling, but never got to the root of the problem.

After Dad died, Mom received hundreds of sympathy cards, and many people reached out to her with flowers, food, and the gift of their time. Even so, she was fearful of other people's condemnation and was keenly aware of what was nonverbally communicated to her by a few people who had heard only Dad's side of the story.

Mom faced the daunting challenge of beginning a new chapter in life. She was already active in ministries, but she increased her involvement. The activity was good for Mom's spirits and served to give her a sense of purpose, but I worried about her always being on the go and not getting enough rest.

Keeping busy had a numbing effect on her pain and distracted her from the persistent loneliness. When she went home, the deafening silence greeted her once again.

Mom went on an antidepressant and started doing better emotionally as time passed. The medication helped her smooth out and enabled us to relate well once again on a consistent basis. Even before Dad died, our relationship had been increasingly marked by conflicts similar to what she and Dad had experienced.

In January 2001, I began to sense a change taking place in Mom's demeanor. She was getting edgy in conversations; she began to slip back into the same behaviors she exhibited before the antidepressant helped her. I was frustrated by what was happening. I enjoyed having a close relationship with Mom similar to the one I had growing up, and I didn't want it to slip away again.

In March, I told Eric something had definitely changed. I guessed that either the medication dosage wasn't effective and needed to be increased or that Mom wasn't taking it anymore.

As I had already learned, dealing with Mom when she was having problems with a chemical imbalance was totally different than dealing with her when it was under control. Each phone call revealed more signs that she was off balance. She was having relational difficulties with others and went back to being critical and suspicious instead of positive and trusting. I knew she was frustrated by her relational problems, but I also knew she wasn't able to face the fact that they were caused by a chemical imbalance.

Dad had often told Mom that their marriage problems were because she was chemically imbalanced. After Dad died, Mom wrongly felt that conceding to a chemical imbalance meant she was in some way responsible for his death. She was in a precarious emotional position. To confront her would bring up a subject she simply couldn't face, and I couldn't do that to her. Yet, I wanted to rescue her from the needless suffering she was enduring. I prayed hard and waited.

One day when Mom and I were talking on the phone, the conversation took an unexpected turn, and I tensed up. I didn't want to have a clash with her.

She suddenly put me on the spot with a very direct question. Answering her question would require that I voice my opinion on what was causing her relational problems. It was as though she knew the truth but wanted and needed to hear me say that it wasn't the case. I cringed and tried to evade the topic, but she became increasingly agitated as I avoided a direct answer. She eventually forced the issue, leaving me no way around it.

I told her about my observations beginning in January and what I'd said to Eric in March. She admitted she had begun to have problematic side effects from the medicine. Sometimes she hadn't been able to complete her sentences or finish her train of thought, so she weaned herself off the medication without the doctor's help or knowledge. The timing of the changes I had seen in her matched the timing of her gradually going off the medication.

I was relieved that the subject was out in the open, and I thought the way was paved for us to have a good talk. I was wrong. Even though Mom recognized the undeniable correlation, she wasn't emotionally able to accept the fact that her relational problems were so closely tied to the medication. She thought if that were true, it would give credence to Dad's accusations that all of their marriage problems were caused by her imbalance.

Dad had been correct about the fact that she had an imbalance and that it affected their relationship. However, he didn't know that Mom had been correct when she said that he too had an imbalance and that it affected their relationship just as much.

Since Dad's opinion was no longer changeable, no matter what new insight might come to light, Mom was sentenced to continue playing the ongoing mind game by herself.

Mom knew she needed help with her worsening depression. Her family doctor started her on a different antidepressant. When her symptoms got worse, he increased the dosage.

Mom's downward spiral resembled a whirlpool sucking more into its grasp as it grew in size and strength. The doctor continued to increase the medicine in an effort to bring her symptoms under control.

One afternoon, one of Mom's friends called to tell me Mom wasn't doing well emotionally or physically. Mom's doctor wanted her to go to a psychiatrist for her medication needs, but because it was going to be awhile before she could be seen, the doctor had increased the dosage again.

Mom asked her friend to call and let me know about her condition because she didn't want to upset me with the news. She felt she was letting Jimmy and me down by not being strong for us. Through it all, she was always concerned about us.

There was a huge factor in Mom's health problems that we were not aware of at the time. We wouldn't find out until autumn that the medication she was taking wasn't right for her. Instead of alleviating her symptoms, it was escalating them. Each dosage increase made her worse. The doctor had mistakenly overlooked that possibility and thought her continually increasing symptoms were from delayed grief and depression. Consequently, Mom kept taking more of the very substance that was causing her health to deteriorate.

As her nervous system took a beating from the medication, Mom picked up more debilitating symptoms. Normal daily living became a challenge for her. She cried often, had panic attacks, couldn't sleep well, and was high-strung and jittery. Soup out of a can became her mainstay for supper, and she lost a lot of weight.

In the midst of everything, Mom kept turning to the Lord. She continued to spend time with Him and asked Him to help her through the depression. Her journals are full of desperate pleas for God's help and guidance, praise to Him for answers to prayer and for who He is, insights from her Bible study or from Christian radio programs, and declarations of her steadfast reliance upon Him.

In mid-August, my high school class had its twentieth reunion at a hotel in Danville, Pennsylvania. Mom was in very bad shape and couldn't handle the pressure of having us stay with her. She felt ashamed that she couldn't, but I understood. It scared me and showed me how debilitating her condition had become.

She still wanted to see us, so I called her when we arrived at our hotel. She was going to spend time with our children for a couple of hours while we were at the reunion and then return home. Our phone conversation was very disturbing. Mom was a wreck—sobbing, indecisive, wanting to come but afraid to do so, apologizing. I tried to give her the emotional freedom to not come if it was too much for her as well as communicate that we wanted to see her if possible. When I hung up, I didn't know what she was going to do. I spoke with her again, and she said she was coming.

I was outside the hotel getting some items from our van when I saw a lady coming toward me across the grass. I had already seen some of my classmates, so I stopped to look intently at the lady to see if she looked familiar. I didn't want to not recognize a classmate, especially not when the lady was the only person around, was less than fifteen feet away, and was heading directly toward me.

Satisfied that I didn't know her, I started to turn away. At that moment, the lady smiled and I was stunned to see my mom's familiar smile. Shocked, I took another look and realized it was indeed Mom. I couldn't believe I had consciously studied her for any hint of familiarity and had not known it was her. Her sunglasses blocked my view of her eyes, but that alone shouldn't have been enough to make me not recognize her.

She had lost so much weight she looked anorexic, even though she wasn't. As I hugged her bony frame, I was appalled at her condition. I wondered how she could have gotten to this point in such a relatively short period of time. Her physical appearance, combined with the talk we had on the phone, left me reeling with disbelief and concern.

One week later I received a phone call from another of Mom's friends telling me that Mom had checked herself into the hospital. The doctor changed her medications, and she immediately began to improve. I was elated by her progress; her appetite returned, and she gained seven pounds in the first two days in the hospital. She took the opportunity to talk to some of the patients about the Lord, and one lady accepted Christ as her Savior.

The hospital released Mom on September 4. That evening she called and was obviously off balance. She was so different from her normal self that it was hard to believe it was the same person at times. She had done well at the beginning of her time in the hospital, but then her medication was changed again. After that, she went downhill. I was incredulous that the doctors had released her instead of keeping her until she was truly stable.

It was obvious to me that the changes made in her medication a couple of days after she improved in the hospital sent her spiraling downward again. Why could I realize what happened just from hearing her in phone conversations from two hundred miles away, yet nobody right there with her figured it out? I was angry and frustrated.

The following day, Mom called in the morning. No reference was made to the previous evening's phone conversation by either of us.

That evening Eric answered the phone when she called around 10:00 PM. She was as off-the-wall as she had been with me the previous evening. Fortunately, she didn't ask to speak with me, and Eric was able to listen to her and try to reassure her of our love. Even though I couldn't hear what Mom was saying, I could tell a lot from Eric's responses. My insides tightened into the familiar knot.

For just over a week, I tried to get in touch with her. She didn't answer the phone or return my calls.

When I finally reached her, I nervously waited to hear what she would say. She began by explaining why she hadn't gotten back to me. She had been busy and out late most nights. I began to relax inside, thinking it might be a good phone call.

All hope went out the window as Mom launched into another totally draining conversation. My insides churned, and a feeling of dread swept over me. I felt physically ill as I listened and prayed.

It was obvious her chemical imbalance was still a problem. I was very frustrated that her doctors had not found the right medication to help her.

Two days later, Mom called to tell me she was in the hospital again. I was scared by the sound of her voice and what she said. This time there wasn't any hint of aggression or verbal attack. Her voice was quiet and flat. The contrast between this latest call and her previous call couldn't have been more pronounced. She sounded defeated and as if she had lost all hope. I was afraid she was going to give up, and I didn't want that to happen.

Around 8:00 PM the same evening, she and I spoke again. I was astonished to hear a difference in her voice. She sounded so much better that I had a hard time believing it was just that morning that she had sounded ready to give up.

The hospital released her two days later. Once again we hoped she was on the right track at last. Only three days later, it was obvious the depression was still overpowering.

By early October, I couldn't find relief from the pressure I felt. The weight of Mom's situation, a CFS relapse, and other problems were taking a toll on me. My emotions were stretched thin in an effort to continue facing the various challenges.

An unexpected phone call on October 6, however, greatly encouraged me and gave me a tremendous emotional boost. Mom and I had a wonderful two-hour conversation. I was so relieved and grateful to the Lord. I desperately wanted my mom back, and that talk was the best one we had enjoyed in a long time. I thought perhaps the correct medication had finally been found and that we were heading in the right direction at last.

On October 25, Mom saw a new family doctor and learned that the antidepressant she had been on had been making her symptoms worse. It had done temporary neurological damage to her system. We were sad to hear what had happened but relieved Mom seemed to be on the right path to reverse her deteriorating health.

A couple days later Mom called, and although she was really struggling, I was relieved that she understood what was going on and wasn't distant or aggressive with me. Only three days later she called at 8:00 AM and was again upset and aggressive. I felt the little energy I had being drained by this latest emotional upheaval.

It was obvious that only the Lord could guide us through the turmoil we were facing. When life is going smoothly, it can be difficult to keep in mind the truth of our total dependence on Him. The hard times serve as reminders of our frailty and His strength. They also provide opportunities for us to practice leaning into Him.

It's very hard to be patient during an uncertain stretch of dark threads when we long for Him to switch colors. Patience is what is needed though, because He knows exactly what He is doing. We haven't been put aside on a forgotten loom in a dark corner; He has us in His hands the whole time.

Chapter 17

Trying to Get Help

SOMETIMES PEOPLE WHO were aware of Mom's struggle with suicidal thoughts tried to encourage me by saying things such as, "Remember, God is sovereign," or, "Just trust God. He's in control." Whenever I heard these and similar statements, I'd think, *I know God is in control, but I also know that things don't always turn out the way I want them to.*

Sometimes we incorrectly think that just because God is in control He won't allow certain things to happen. But we live in a sinful, broken world, and many of the painful things that take place don't make sense to us.

Consider Job. The horrendous things he went through happened because of a conversation between Satan and God. Satan was convinced that if Job went through some hard times, he would put his opinion of God up for review and turn his back on God. So God set the parameters of what Satan was allowed to do, and the trials began. Job underwent tremendous suffering and didn't have a clue why it was happening. His quiet life of enjoyed prosperity ended abruptly when his children, material goods, lifestyle, and health were taken away almost simultaneously.

The depth and breadth of Job's intense suffering was magnified by heaven's silence. Job's wife advised him to turn his back on God. Even so, in the middle of it all, Job voiced something I'm sure was a blow to Satan but put a smile on God's face when he said, "Though he slay me, yet will I hope in him" (Job 13:15).

I have found that trusting God has a lot more to do with continuing to believe the truths about Him found in His Word when we are in the midst of painful trials than with believing He will always prevent them from happening or divinely intervene. God didn't create us as robots and program us to love and trust Him always. Instead, He gave us free will to choose to continue to love and trust Him, even when life hurts.

My brother, Jimmy, and I stayed in contact with each other and tried to keep a handle on Mom's condition. We were both afraid of what she might do and often talked about it. We didn't want to lose her, especially to suicide.

On November 20, I called Mom to see how she was doing. At first she seemed to be doing well. Eventually she made a comment that caused some concern, so I followed up with a question. Her answer was a verbal red flag.

I questioned her more directly and was aghast at her answers. I realized the roadblocks Mom had built to separate her from committing suicide had already been taken down. I wondered what had kept her from already taking that step.

I knew she was actively suicidal. I was two hundred miles away with only a phone to connect us, and I knew I had to risk getting off the phone to get help to her.

After securing a promise that she wouldn't do anything to herself, I told her I would call right back as soon as I reached someone. I was afraid to trust her to keep her promise, but I was equally afraid not to get help to her immediately.

I hung up the phone and started dialing numbers. I wasn't able to reach anyone close to her. I finally reached Aunt Mary, Mom's sister. I told her what was going on, and she said she and Uncle Bill were on their way. I was relieved help was coming, but I knew it would take some time for them to make the forty-minute trip.

I dialed Mom's number again, praying she would answer, and she did. I told her Aunt Mary and Uncle Bill were on their way. I kept her talking, praying she wouldn't hang up on me before they got there.

I never asked how fast Uncle Bill drove that night, but he must have been flying. When Mom told me they were in the driveway, I couldn't believe they were there so quickly. I was grateful to the Lord they were able to take such immediate action.

That evening, we decided Mom couldn't be alone until she was able to see a new psychiatrist on November 30. The logical place for her to stay until then was our house. We readily agreed to have her stay with us for those ten days.

As I prepared for Mom's visit, I realized I needed to hide her Christmas gift. I had found a soft black chenille hat, scarf, and gloves set for her. When I picked it up, a strange thought passed through my mind, *You'll get to wrap her present, but she won't live long enough to open it.* I wondered if God was preparing me as He had with Dad.

Mom arrived the next morning. She was in such bad shape that I wondered how she had been able to drive. I put my arms around her, and she began to sob.

The next ten days were emotionally intense. Mom was valiant in her continual effort not to break down, but it was a lost cause. She didn't want to upset us with her crying episodes. Each time she broke down, she apologized, even though we repeatedly told her there wasn't anything wrong with crying.

A couple days after Thanksgiving, Mom and I were on the way to a store when she suddenly paled and said we needed to get home quickly. I thought she was getting sick.

After we were home, she began to feel some better. I asked her if she thought she was getting sick. She told me that she had been fighting self-destructive thoughts that day. They were the worst ones she had experienced, and she feared she was going out of her mind. She looked at me with such fear and sadness. Her eyes begged me to understand and do something to deliver her from the horror she was enduring. I felt helpless.

I was also angry. I was losing my mom slowly, but surely. *Why hasn't someone been able to help her? How can doctors play around with her medicine and not be able to observe the results of their experiments? She isn't a guinea pig! She has actively sought help, and it's gotten her nowhere—worse than nowhere. It's brought her to this all-time low.* I was afraid she wouldn't be able to return from the depths to which she had plunged.

The stress of watching Mom hurting so much ate away at all of us. Most of the time she was weepy, but she also had times of being edgy and aggressive. One of those times turned into an uncomfortable interaction for both of us. We had a strained conversation, and I had to leave for an appointment immediately after we were done talking. When I got back, Mom's van was missing. I wondered where she had gone, so I went to Benjamin's bedroom and asked him. She had told him she was going for a walk. I told him her van was gone, and then raced upstairs to search for her belongings. Sure enough, she had packed up and left.

I was very upset and didn't know what I should do. I knew our conversation had troubled her, but I hadn't expected her to leave. The situation was so complicated by a multitude of factors that I didn't know where to begin.

Did she leave town, or is she just out there driving around? Is she suicidal at the moment? Why would she have taken her belongings if she had left intent on committing suicide? Should I go out and drive around looking for her? Where would she go? Should I call the police? Even if she's on her way home, something has to be done, because she can't be left alone; it's too risky.

I prayed and asked the Lord to show me what to do and to help in the situation. He knew exactly where she was and what state of mind she was in. I prayed for His protection over her.

The telephone ring startled me. I was relieved when I heard Mom's voice. She said she was going home and was at a rest stop forty-five minutes south of Rochester. I told her she needed to come back. She said she was going to be leaving the following day anyhow to get home for the appointment. She was just going a day earlier. It would give her enough time to get unpacked and settled in. I responded that she could unpack in very little time and had no need to go home that day. I told her she couldn't stay by herself, no matter what she thought. I again told her she needed to come back and said if she didn't turn around right away I would call the state police with a description of her and her vehicle. That finally convinced her; I felt bad that I had to talk to my mom that way.

I was eager for Mom to see the new psychiatrist. He came highly recommended by a counselor she had started seeing. I expected him to admit her and keep her there until she was stabilized. That would be a tremendous relief for Jimmy and me! We were very aware of our inability to prevent Mom from committing suicide, no matter how hard we worked to try to stop it. I had high hopes that we were approaching a turning point in the situation and that we were finally going to head the right direction.

Mom saw her counselor the day she was going to see the psychiatrist. She admitted her suicidal thinking. Her counselor was concerned about Mom and was glad she was going directly to the psychiatrist's office when she left their session.

When Mom called to tell me about her appointment, I expected her to say she was in the hospital. She wasn't. The psychiatrist had changed her medication and allowed her to go home. I was dumbfounded. I didn't understand why he hadn't admitted her.

The pressure was rising on all fronts. Mom's situation was grave, and my health seesawed precariously. As we went through each day, we continued to ask God to intervene in the trials we were facing. We longed for relief on at least one front.

A bit of relief came on December 5 when Mom left three good messages for us. We thought maybe the new medicine was going to be the answer to righting her imbalance.

A week later, I had another difficult call from her. Two days later, I realized she was very close to committing suicide.

The following morning, Aunt Mary and Jimmy took Mom back to the hospital where she was admitted. I was relieved to know she was relatively safe in the hospital, but I was frustrated with the entire mental-health treatment protocol.

The practice of admitting a patient and evaluating their needs over several weeks to determine and implement the right course of action was not to be found. Insurance companies put financial interests above patient care, and patients are on the losing end. Hospitalization is used as a brief stabilizing period, sometimes followed by day treatment called partial programs. Personnel want patients to receive the help they need in daily six-hour sessions on an out-patient basis, so they don't offer the type of in-patient programs some people need. Either a person is hospitalized and faces the majority of his or her day without any structured program or isn't hospitalized in order to have access to the partial program. For a suicidal person, that can be a lethal choice. It's a predicament no one should ever have to face.

Christmas was getting close, and I felt bad that Mom was going to be in the hospital. I wanted to see her, but the trip would take the whole day, and I needed to think about my family also.

I wanted Christmas to be the enjoyable celebration of Jesus' birth that it normally is at our house. We needed the stability of our traditions to offset the upheaval and uncertainty that permeated our lives. I knew I needed to put my family first and maintain as much normalcy as possible.

As I went through each day, I tried to remain outwardly enthusiastic when the children were around. I didn't want them to be any more negatively affected than they already were.

I mentally flipped between living in the present and remembering previous Christmas celebrations. My parents had always made Christmas special for us, and I wanted to do the same for my children.

On Christmas Eve, we were eating our traditional meal of subs, pizza, pickled herring, and munchies when Mom called from the hospital. I slipped upstairs to our bedroom so I could have a quiet place to talk. I was sad that she was in the hospital instead of being with us.

Downstairs, Eric and the children were laughing and having a good time enjoying each other. Mom was two hundred miles away in a cheerless, impersonal room with strangers, as families all over the world celebrated Christ's birth.

After the children went to bed, Eric and I sat on the couch. The Christmas tree lights were the only lights in the room. In the silence, I tried to set aside the stressful thoughts in my mind and redirect my focus to living in the moment. I snuggled into Eric's shoulder and thanked God for getting me through the day. I realized how much I had to be grateful for in the midst of everything going on and that it all flowed from the hand of my faithful and loving God.

Chapter 18

Fearing and Hearing the Worst

CHRISTMAS MORNING WAS the typical flurry of activity. We sang "Happy Birthday" to Jesus, opened presents, emptied stockings, and ate our traditional brunch of baked eggs, sausage, stollen, and orange wedges. My thoughts kept shifting between my family in the living room and Mom in the hospital.

The children enjoyed our time together, and it was a mostly relaxing day. That night I was very grateful to the Lord for having brought me through it.

New Year's brought the usual sense of newness and a fresh start. I hoped the worst was behind us and that the new year would be less stressful. That was not to be.

On January 2, we learned that Eric's sister, Gail, had a rare type of cancer on her tongue.

The following day, the OB/GYN told me I needed to have a laparoscopy. I told him I didn't have time for surgery.

The next day, Friday, Mom was released from the hospital. Aunt Mary drove her home. Mom wasn't doing well; she was anxious and experiencing panic attacks.

Part of Mom's treatment plan was for her to go to a partial program at the hospital. She was supposed to start on Monday; however, a snowstorm prevented her from making the one-hour drive that morning.

That evening, Jimmy called me to say he was worried. He had stopped by Mom's house and found the house open, the lights on, and

Mom missing. He had already searched the house and found her Last Will and Testament set out in plain sight instead of in its normal place in the safe. Her van was in the usual spot in the first bay of the pole barn. The window was rolled down a bit, and it smelled like fumes inside.

With that news, I guessed what had happened. She had intended to commit suicide using the car fumes, but changed her mind and walked away from the situation to remove herself from the temptation. She was physically too weak to have walked far. There weren't footprints in the deep snow around the house, so she must have gone down the road.

I realized she had probably walked the short distance to Jimmy's landlady's house because they were good friends. Jimmy hung up the phone to find out if we had guessed right.

He called back and told me that he found Mom playing cards with his landlady. She acted as though nothing had happened. He told her he needed to talk to her before she went to bed.

When Mom called him, he went to her house and confronted her with the evidence that she had walked away from committing suicide. She began to cry.

Jimmy called me right away. His voice was constricted as he choked out, "It was another aborted attempt." My heart plunged. She had been released only three days before!

I could hear Mom crying and pleading with Jimmy not to admit her to the hospital. Jimmy knew she needed to be protected from herself.

He got off the phone in order to make some calls. When he called back, I could hear Mom still crying. We were both relieved that Aunt Mary came to help. Jimmy made more calls using his cell phone while he had me on Mom's home phone. I tried to hear what he was saying over the sound of Mom crying, but I could tell the process of trying to get Mom admitted wasn't going well.

Jimmy was finally able to speak with the same man at the hospital he had spoken with for Mom's previous admission. He explained what happened and told him he wanted to admit her. The man refused. He told Jimmy that she needed to be in the partial program. Jimmy told him she would commit suicide if he didn't admit her, and that he couldn't watch her 24/7. The man replied that if the people running the program thought she was at risk, they would address it. Jimmy literally begged him to admit her. The man's final response was to tell Jimmy that it was not Jimmy's decision to make, it was his. He refused to allow Jimmy to admit her.

I was incredulous when Jimmy filled me in. Mom had just walked away from an attempt in progress, was hysterical, and the man wouldn't allow us to admit her. I couldn't believe he was preventing us from getting her to a safe place.

Jimmy said he was going to get off the phone and help Aunt Mary try to get Mom calmed down.

It took some time before Aunt Mary was able to call and update me. Mom had stopped crying and was in a better state of mind. Aunt Mary had a cautious optimism that she would be okay, even though she hadn't been admitted.

She said that Mom was hysterical at the possibility of being hospitalized, and she was afraid that if she had been admitted Mom might have had a complete mental breakdown. That thought had already crossed my mind, and I shared her concern. I had never heard anyone sound so out of control. I felt that it was a very real possibility, but I also feared she would commit suicide if she wasn't admitted. I didn't want either of those things to happen, and neither did Aunt Mary.

One thing we did know for sure: the decision had been taken out of our hands, and the course had been set by the man who wouldn't allow us to admit her. I was aware that from that night on only one way could be played out to the end, and the man on the phone had chosen the way. We never would know what the consequences of admitting her would have been. We would find out only what the consequences of not admitting her would be. Moreover, there wouldn't be any going back to change the outcome.

Even though I still feared for Mom's life, I tried to take hope in Aunt Mary's cautious optimism. Maybe Mom would be okay, and the partial program would help her. Maybe we were close to Mom finally getting the help she needed. Time would tell.

Eric's sister, Gail, had extensive surgery to remove the cancer in her tongue on January 16. We waited and prayed throughout the day, watching the hours tick by. We finally received the phone call we were waiting for. Gail had made it through a very invasive procedure. It would be a long recovery, but the surgery was behind her. We breathed a sigh of relief. At least there was good news on that front.

One area of life that overwhelmed Mom was her paperwork. Normally a very organized person, she had fallen behind in keeping up with it. She brought some paperwork with her when she visited in November, and I had worked on it then. There was more to do though, so I planned to go to Pennsylvania the upcoming weekend to help her.

I knew she wasn't eating well, so I had made meals and frozen them to take with me. I had enough food for the two of us for the weekend, plus meals to leave with her. We confirmed our plans Thursday night.

Friday, January 18, 2002, was a cold day. I was taking a shower when my eight-year-old, Daniel, knocked on the bathroom door saying I had a phone call from Nana. I was surprised that she was calling at that time. I thought it was odd she would already have a break only thirty minutes into the partial program.

Mom told me she was home. She said she was sorry, but we had to put off my trip to see her. She had become ill on her way to the program and returned home. She thought it was a twenty-four-hour stomach virus and mentioned that someone in the program had just had the same thing.

I offered to come later in the day or the next morning. She said she wasn't sure she would be better by then and that we should wait for another time. I agreed to check my calendar to see if I could come the following weekend. I told her to drink lots of water and get some rest and I would call and check on her in the afternoon.

Once I was ready for the day, I found myself in the unusual position of having some free time on my hands. I didn't need to have school, because I had worked ahead and had completed that day's work in anticipation of being at Mom's. The house needed attention, so I decided to do some cleaning.

Hours later, I went upstairs and was getting a dust cloth out of the linen closet when a strange thought passed through my mind. I was looking down the stairs at the living room when I thought, *Did the Lord allow me the time to get all this cleaning done because He knows Mom is going to commit suicide today and people are going to come to the house tonight?* I wondered if it was the Lord putting the idea in my head and if He was preparing me beforehand as He had before Dad's death. It was an unsettling thought.

That afternoon around 4:00 PM, I stopped what I was doing to call Mom. She didn't answer. I thought she might be soaking in a tub of vinegar water, something she often did when she didn't feel well. I waited about ten minutes and called again. Still no answer.

A feeling of dread came over me the first time Mom didn't answer, and the feeling deepened with each unanswered call. I leaned against the kitchen counter and stared at a picture on the refrigerator across the room. Mom's smiling face looked back at me from the four-generation photo of Gram, Mom, Naomi, and me.

I continued to call and pray. *Is she dead? Am I going to forever remember leaning against the counter looking at the picture? Am I going to eventually listen to my own messages on her voice mail because I'll be at her house taking care of what needs to be done in the wake of her death?*

Remnants of my legalistic background reappeared. I could hear people saying, "Now, Maureen, you shouldn't worry about your mom. Just trust God. Worry is sin. Don't borrow trouble. You don't know that anything has happened, so don't worry. Just pray and commit her to Him. She's in His hands, isn't she? Worry doesn't honor God."

I knew that type of thinking was based on the assumption that God won't allow bad things to happen if we just trust Him. God *does* allow bad things to happen, and sometimes fear accompanies them. God doesn't owe it to us to deliver us from our suffering, and He isn't a magic genie who can be manipulated to grant our wish and make everything turn out the way we tell Him we want it to.

After all, He is the great I AM (Exodus 3:13–14), and doesn't need to answer to mere mortals. Psalm 89:6–7 says, "For who in the skies above can compare with the LORD? Who is like the LORD among the heavenly beings? In the council of the holy ones God is greatly feared; he is more awesome than all who surround him."

God's ways can't be compared to man's ways. He alone knows and understands everything. His works are great, and His thoughts are deep (Psalm 92:5).

When we face trials, we need to focus on the One who will go with us through them. We need to keep putting our trust in Him and continue to believe He loves us, even though painful circumstances try to convince us otherwise.

In Psalm 143, David records his desperate plea for God's help. He honestly admits his feelings, and he remembers what God had already done for him in the past. He then implores the Lord for help and places his trust in Him.

I knew I needed to do the same thing in dealing with Mom. With Dad, I hadn't had any warning on the day of his death. My interactions with the Lord about Dad's suicide all came after I knew he was dead. This situation was different. I already knew there was a good possibility that my mom had committed suicide. I thought of the fact that God knew exactly where she was and how she was. He could see her, and He could see me. He knew the truth of the situation.

Has she already committed suicide? Is she already with You? Is she already free from the depression and panic attacks and all the things she's suffered with for so long, and I just don't know she's gone yet? Is that what I'm going to find out?

As I continued to dial her number without any response, my heart was full of fear. I tried to think of a benign explanation for her absence, but knew I was grasping at straws. Deep down I knew there wasn't one. I knew she would never have left the house without calling me, because she knew I would be afraid if I called and she didn't answer.

I had left a message on Jimmy's answering machine telling him I couldn't get a hold of Mom. I asked him to check on her as soon as he heard the message. An hour and a half passed, and I still didn't hear from Jimmy.

I wondered if I should call the state police, but I hesitated to do that, because I knew my grandparents often listened to their scanner. I didn't want them to hear a dispatcher sending police to their daughter's home.

Then I thought of a different idea. I called Jimmy's landlady. She lived within sight of Mom's house. I didn't want to alarm her unnecessarily, so I tried to sound casual as I asked if she could normally see Mom's van when it was in the pole barn. She said she could. I asked her to look to see if it was there. She left the phone to check. When she returned, she said it wasn't there and asked if I would like her to go up to Mom's and check to make sure. Relieved and surprised, I declined her offer and thanked her for her help. While I was glad she couldn't see the van, I also wondered if Mom had moved it where it couldn't be seen as part of her plan. Or maybe it was there, but the neighbor couldn't see it for some reason. At any rate, I didn't want to risk sending the neighbor up to check things out in case Mom had committed suicide.

Since the van couldn't be seen, I decided against calling the state police and went back to hoping there was an explanation for her absence I hadn't thought of yet. By that time, almost two and a half hours had gone by since I had made the first phone call to Mom. I kept calling. Each time I listened to the familiar sound of the ringing and ached to hear her voice on the other end. I let it ring many times, not wanting to hang up again.

Jimmy finally called. He had just gotten home and heard my message. He told me he was going up right away. The sound of his voice was reassuring. Maybe things would be okay after all. Jimmy wasn't flipping out like I was. Of course, he hadn't been trying to call her for two and a half hours either.

A few minutes later, the phone rang again. It was Jimmy. He tersely asked me if Eric was there. I told him he was, and he told me to put him on the phone. When Eric picked up the other extension, Jimmy told me to hang up the phone. I was already afraid because of the sound of his voice. The fact that he wanted me off the phone sent a wave of sheer terror through me. I started to argue with him about hanging up, but he cut in with a forceful, "Reen, hang up the phone, now!" I hung up. I prayed. I reached for the phone. I pulled my hand back. I prayed. A couple of minutes passed, and I couldn't take it any longer. I grabbed the phone and pressed the receiver to my ear. I heard Jimmy reading what was obviously the end of a note. He said it was taped to the back door. The part I heard him read told him not to come in but to call Bruce McMichael at the funeral home.

My heart was pounding hard. Our worst fear had become reality. The fact that she hadn't answered the phone confirmed she had gone through with her attempt. Even knowing that much, I still hoped she was alive. Jimmy said he was going into the house to find her. Without saying it, we both thought she probably had taken an overdose of the medication she was on. If so, Jimmy knew there might be a chance he could save her. From his experience with the fire department, he knew he could have Life Flight on the ground nearby in a matter of minutes.

Jimmy said he would call us back. We waited for what seemed an eternity. I jumped when the phone rang. He had found her. He was on his cell phone with the state police. I asked if she was dead. He said he wasn't 100 percent sure, but he thought so.

Not again! Not Mom too! It just had to be a horrendous nightmare. Surely I would wake up and find that it really hadn't happened!

I clung tenaciously to the faint hope that she wasn't dead. That hope soon was snuffed out when a state trooper confirmed her death. She was gone.

Over the phone, the background sounds of troopers talking, police radios crackling, and people moving around in the kitchen enabled me to picture the scene unfolding in the house.

I tried to absorb the reality of what had occurred, but my head felt swollen and heavy. Shock was already enfolding me with its blessed numbing blanket.

Chapter 19

Grieving Another Suicide

AS THE NEWS of Mom's death spread, friends began to arrive. Once again, God used our church family to introduce brightly colored threads into our tapestry. Their warm embraces, words of condolence, loving concern, and prayer support comforted us. At one point, I remembered the thought I had earlier about the Lord allowing me to clean the house because He knew Mom was going to commit suicide and people would come that night. He did it again. He went before and began to prepare me for her death.

After everyone except Carol Cassara left, we needed to pack to leave in the morning. Eric and I went to Naomi's room to see how she was doing. Our three-and-a-half-year-old was sound asleep with Carol next to her. Carol joined us in the hallway. Her presence introduced another bright thread at a very dark time.

My head felt so thick that I found it hard to think straight. I couldn't process my thoughts well. Carol took over for me. She asked questions about what needed to be done. Whenever I couldn't think, she supplied the answer. She took the lead and got suitcases from the basement, then talked me through picking out clothes. Steadily we began to assemble everything we needed. The hours went by.

At 1:30 AM, Carol, Benjamin, and I sat on the living-room floor and went through pictures. When everything was done and we were ready for our trip, Carol embraced us warmly, assured us of her prayers, and went home.

The following morning we stopped at church to pick up Daniel, who had attended a Stockade sleepover. I waited in the car. Gregg Terry came outside to express his condolences. God used Gregg as another bright-colored thread. He didn't allow the awkwardness associated with suicide to prevent him from reaching out to me. I told him that the pastor in Benton was going to find housing for us. I was reluctant to stay with anyone, but we needed somewhere to stay. After listening to my concerns, he prayed for the Lord to give us the perfect place.

The trip down was surreal. We traveled the same road we had traveled for seventeen years, yet we weren't going to the same place. Instead of eagerly anticipating getting home, we didn't even know where we were going to stay. I thought about the fact that Mom's home remained unchanged visually, but it was no longer the same. Without the life and love of the two who had once lived there, their inviting home had become an empty house. Memories flooded my tired mind, and I was swept away in the current, too tired to fight it.

When we got to the church, the pastor led us to the place where we would stay. My heart began to relax a bit as we followed his car. The way to the apartment was part of what had been my school bus route. As we passed the familiar fields and woods, I thought about the time in my life when my parents were both alive and I felt secure in the love of a tight-knit family.

As we turned off the route and traveled the final half mile, I was overcome with gratefulness to the Lord. The beautiful scenery soothed my soul. Heavy laden evergreen branches bowing low under thick white blankets lined the road. Large fluffy flakes floated gently down to find their rest on the ground.

The Lord provided a wonderful place for us in answer to Gregg's prayer. The owners made us feel at home and then gave us space to be ourselves and not have to interact with anyone. We stayed in an apartment above a detached garage far enough away from the house to give complete privacy.

People from church had brought some basic food items in anticipation of our arrival. A young lady who had worked with Mom in the Awana program stopped by long enough to drop off cold cuts, chips, bread, and soup for us. I hadn't even thought about food. Their thoughtfulness and kindness in anticipating our need and taking time to look out for us were light-colored threads in the tapestry. I was grateful for the visible evidence of God's loving faithfulness.

Saturday was a blur of activity. Jimmy and I went through the motions, running on adrenaline. We planned the funeral service and arranged to meet at church with the two pastors who were to participate in it. Jimmy filled me in on the arrangements he had made at McMichael's funeral home with Aunt Mary's help. They had also taken care of ordering flowers for the casket.

Aunt Mary's presence and assistance was another light-colored thread God wove into a dark area of the tapestry. She not only helped in tangible ways, but we knew she shared the heartache of losing Mom on a level that was uniquely felt by family. Aunt Mary and Uncle Bill served as a link to our common past and a stabilizing force when our world once again spun out of control.

In the afternoon, I gave Eric and the boys haircuts, settled the remaining details for the viewing and funeral, and made numerous phone calls.

That evening after getting our children settled in, Eric and I finally went to bed. Exhaustion didn't prevent the harsh reality of Mom's death from penetrating my foggy brain. The unfamiliar surroundings taunted me as they loudly proclaimed that even though I was in Benton, I wasn't home. Many thoughts and emotions fought for my attention, pushing their way to the forefront of my consciousness, only to be knocked aside before I could address them. I wanted to shut my eyes and awaken in my own bed at my parents' house. Sleep eventually rescued me.

Sunday morning I went to Mom's house early. I was going to meet Aunt Mary there and look through the large sea chest containing family pictures. I wanted to add to the ones I already had.

Driving up the familiar driveway was a difficult experience. How could everything look so normal when such a terrible tragedy had taken place two days before? The element of familiarity was deceitful as it evoked a sense of hope that Mom would walk out of the house with her cheery greeting, just like she had always done. Even as I hoped that would happen, I knew better. The events of the previous two days were permanently burned in my mind and heart. It was no dream. Now both

Dad and Mom were gone, and there was no changing that. Nobody was going to greet me when I got out of the car—not today, not ever. The emotional impact from the weight of reality was crushing. The utter finality of a relationship and way of life I had always known and cherished at that very place began to sink in.

As I entered the house, the silence was deafening. My eyes took in the familiar objects. How could everything be the same, and yet be so totally different? It was like being on a prepared stage with all the props in place waiting to film the next episode in an ongoing series. The only problem was the lead actress was missing. Without her, the show couldn't go on. It was over. Not only was it over, but Jimmy and I were the stage crew responsible for disassembling the props. I didn't want to be part of the stage crew. I wanted to be part of the cast and live out another scene with Mom.

I slowly made my way through the downstairs, letting my eyes soak in each familiar detail. My heart desperately clung to the warm feelings of familiarity and sought to find comfort in them until I realized that comfort wasn't what I truly desired. What I really wanted was to find a way to turn time back to when the house was our home and we were together. I wanted to remove the gaping chasm between us.

Memories of the sound of happy voices deceived me into feeling that my loved ones were tantalizingly close. Then the loud voices of memory softened, and the silence quietly enveloped me with its harsh evidence of reality.

Suddenly my eyes locked on an object that made me feel as though Mom simply had to be alive. Her blue cardigan with brown wooden buttons was draped over the back of a dining-room chair as though she had left it there just moments before. I quickly went around the table and hugged the chair and the cardigan on it, crying out, "Oh, Mom!" My mind toyed with the thought that perhaps it was only a dream or that Mom was really upstairs using the restroom. Once again, reality shattered my intense desire.

A neatly folded pile of Mom's clothes was on the deacon's bench against the wall. I put my arms around the entire pile, hugging it at first and then burying my face to smell the familiar scent that remained. I lifted my head slightly and inhaled deeply in an effort to lock the memory of that moment in my mind. I wished I could capture the smell and keep it in a jar like perfume. Eventually, I relaxed my grip and walked through the rest of the house.

Aunt Mary arrived with her brother, Uncle John. I was glad to see both of them and was thankful for their presence and help. I knew Mom's death was hard on them too, and I appreciated their willingness to come to the house to help me.

The three of us went through photos in the living room until we felt we had as many as we needed. Aunt Mary had some of Mom as a child. We mounted most of them on poster board and left the rest for the magnetic board at the funeral home.

As I went down the driveway, I was aware of the fact that God had shown His faithful love to me by providing Mom's sister and brother to help me do a difficult task.

We arrived at the funeral home early. Our good friend, Tony Cassara, greeted us in the parking lot. He had driven down from Rochester to attend the viewing and the funeral. What a comfort it was to see him there! His warm embrace and supportive presence was another gift from God. He handed us two six-hundred-minute prepaid phone call cards to help with the many calls he knew we were making.

Tony's presence also provided a sense of stability for me. Even though everything had changed for me in Benton, Tony provided a visible reminder of the church family we still had in Rochester. Through Tony, more bright-colored threads were introduced.

The services were held at the same funeral home that Dad's had been. I had never been there, but I recognized it from the pictures Eric had taken for me at Dad's viewing.

As I walked into the room, it felt unreal. *Mom should be with us. Aren't we here today for Dad's viewing? Our family can't be down to just Jimmy and me, can it? How did this happen to us? Jimmy and I should be up at the house with both Dad and Mom, enjoying each other's company, instead of being at the funeral home for Mom's viewing.*

The owner of the funeral home, Bruce McMichael, was one of Dad's former students. When I was a kid, Bruce worked in the small IGA store on Main Street. I could still picture him as a teenager, wearing his white apron and working behind the cash register and sweeping the aisles. Who would have thought then that he would end up owning a funeral home and be the one to take care of Dad's and Mom's funerals?

As I went around the room, setting out photos, Bruce and I talked. He expressed his sympathy and spoke of his own struggle to work through what had happened. He said, "I'm still not over your dad's death, and now this." He recalled when Mom approached him after a graveside service for a local man. She told him she and Dad had decided Bruce would handle the arrangements for their funerals when they died. Bruce thought it would be a long time before that happened, since they were both so young. It happened far too soon.

Our conversation was so different than the stereotypical interaction between an emotionless funeral director and a weeping family member grieving over the loss of someone the director never met. Our conversation was a friend-to-friend talk expressing our shared loss. It was a great comfort to me. I was startled to realize that the Lord was graciously allowing me to have my own "belated funeral" for my dad in the very room where his real funeral had taken place more than three years earlier. As Bruce expressed his thoughts and feelings, I was grateful for his compassionate presence. His genuine sorrow and willingness to talk with me so honestly was a precious gift from God. I marveled that God was using even the funeral-home setting to reach out to me and to introduce bright-colored threads.

People started coming half an hour early, and there was a steady line until well after it was supposed to be over. Standing up for hours was hard, but the Lord gave me the strength to get through it.

As person after person passed by, the impact of Mom's life on others was evident. Immediate and extended family, many of her former classmates, our retired family dentist, church friends, people from Benton, teachers, neighbors, people for whom Mom had worked, people from the Millville community where she had grown up, and a host of others whose lives she had touched waited in line outside in the bitter cold until they could enter the building.

Part way through the evening, I needed to use the restroom, but I didn't want to leave the line and miss people. The Lord even took care of that for me. I looked at the line snaking its way toward me from the right side to see if there might be a break when I could leave and not be missed. There was no end in sight, but I did notice a long string of people in uniform. It was the fire department. I was glad for Jimmy to have such a thoughtful display of support, and it provided the perfect opportunity.

I made my way to the back of the room, trying not to catch anyone's eye so as not to get detained. As I lifted my eyes so I could cut through the line of people, I saw my sister-in-law, Grace, and her family. When I came out of the restroom, Grace was waiting for me in the hallway. She gave me a hug and quickly prayed with me. I knew the Lord was reaching out to me again, and I marveled at His orchestration of events to bring about our brief, encouraging time together.

At the end of the viewing, Eric's brother, Nathan, ministered to us in music. His spontaneous offer to sing was another way the Lord reached out to me. Hearing Gram's voice as we sang the hymns was comforting. It brought back memories of singing in church as well as of her playing the organ and singing at home. I was grateful for any experience that was somewhat familiar as my mind tried to right its awful spinning and regain a stable footing once again.

After we finished, we went back to the apartment and put the children to bed. I had one more task to do. I needed to write my tribute for the funeral service. I asked God to help me and began working on it at 10:00. I couldn't think of a way to begin. I kept jotting down ideas and crossing them out.

Finally, I told the Lord that I was still going to wait on Him because I couldn't do it on my own, but that it was getting late and I really needed some sleep, so I really needed Him to help me soon. An idea came to my mind. I wrote down categories about topics I wanted to include in my talk. Just before 11:00 PM I began to write. I finished just before 3:00 AM but couldn't fall asleep until around four o'clock. When the alarm went off at 7:00 AM, I wondered how I was going to get by on only three hours of sleep. I knew that God would need to give me the strength.

When we arrived at the funeral home, we saw more friends from Rochester, Tom and Linda Cribbs, who had driven down that morning for the funeral. Their loving support introduced another bright-colored thread into our tapestry. We were grateful for their presence, as well as for everyone who took the time to attend.

Reading the tribute was important to me, especially since I hadn't been able to attend Dad's funeral. However, I didn't know if I would be able to get through it.

Before the service began, many people greeted us. As fellow believers talked to me, I asked them to pray for me to get through the talk.

Not too far into giving the tribute, I was afraid I wouldn't be able to continue. Then I thought, *Yes you will! West Side is praying, and so are many people here right now.* The panicky feeling left, and I finished without any problems.

Afterwards, I was so thankful for God's guidance in writing it and for His strength in delivering it. Many people commented on what I had written, and I was able to tell them that the Lord was the One who helped me.

After the funeral, we went to the cemetery. The biting cold wind wrapped its arms around each person who braved the snowy conditions to be with us. I sat next to Jimmy, who was shaking in his suit coat. Someone gave him a winter coat to wrap around his shoulders. I looked across the top of the casket and stared at our cousins serving as pallbearers. We had shared such happy times growing up, and now we were huddled in the below-freezing temperatures around a freshly dug grave to bury Mom. *What happened in the years since our childhood? How did we get to this place?*

After we left the graveyard, we went to the social hall at the Bible Baptist Church for a funeral luncheon. I wanted to go to every table to thank each person for coming, but I needed to eat. After lunch, Naomi didn't feel well. Taking care of her occupied my time, and before I knew it, people were leaving and I hadn't gotten to talk with them. I felt bad that I hadn't thanked them and felt that I had let them down.

While people were cleaning up, Tony Cassara received a text message from his wife, Carol. Our neighbor, Kathy Keyes, had offered to watch the children during the day if Eric wanted to come home earlier than I did. We decided to send the boys back to Rochester with Tony and to keep Naomi with us.

On their way home, Tony stopped at a mall in the southern tier and took the boys to a Chinese restaurant. Daniel loved the crab legs.

Carol arranged to have a young couple, Rob and Stefanie Sierk, stay with Benjamin and Daniel in the evenings until we went back home. The boys loved it, and it was a tremendous blessing to us.

Before they left to go back to Rochester, Tom and Linda asked if there was anything they could do to help us. Linda asked if we needed any groceries. I couldn't picture the inside of my refrigerator. When I closed my eyes to concentrate, all I could see was the inside of Mom's refrigerator. Linda quickly perceived my inability to think straight and told me not to worry about it. She said she would check it out when they got back and would make sure the kids had everything they needed. When she asked if there was anything else she could do, I suddenly remembered the food I had made to take to Mom's. I didn't want to see it in the freezer when I got home. I told Linda about it and she said she would take care of it for me.

When we rejoined the boys in Rochester, we were exhausted physically and emotionally, but there was no time to rest. Eric went back to work, and there was much to be done in the couple of days before we returned to Benton for the weekend.

My head felt swollen, as though it had been overstuffed with cotton. I envisioned it looking like an overgrown cauliflower. The physical sensation of being swollen was so strong that there were times I wondered why people weren't staring at me like I was a sideshow exhibit in a circus. Mentally processing anything took longer than normal. It felt as though the world had caved in around me, and I needed to dig out of the debris that pressed in on all sides.

That Friday I needed to pack and meet Eric when his workday ended. My head felt thick and heavy. I had no energy, and I was having dizzy spells. I kept trying to accomplish something, but had to keep sitting down to let the dizziness pass.

In the early afternoon, two friends from church, Patricia Regelsberger and Cindy Capuano, stopped by with a fruit and goodies basket from our church family. Cindy also brought some leftover split-pea soup. It was only enough for one person, but she brought what she had, apologizing that it wasn't more. It was the perfect amount for me, and I love split-pea soup.

The two of them realized I was in sad shape and offered to help. Patricia gave Naomi a bath and got her ready to go. Cindy cleaned up the kitchen and helped me pack. We finished getting ready right on time for me to leave. I couldn't have done it without their help.

Patricia drove us to meet Eric so I didn't have to drive with the dizziness. Then she drove the car Eric had taken to work back to our house so we didn't have to pick it up on our way home. She even filled the gas tank.

Carol arranged for the boys to be taken care of again that weekend. The Sierks watched them Friday, and John and Lin Lohman watched them Saturday and Sunday.

Carol also coordinated meals for our family for a few weeks. I don't know how we would have gotten through those days without the help and support of our church family.

Checking for basics in a refrigerator, removing something from a freezer, childcare, help packing, a single serving of leftover soup, a trip to a Chinese restaurant and a little boy's delight in eating crab legs, organizing meals, giving a ride, and topping off a gas tank might not sound like impressive ways for God to reveal Himself, but that's how He works. He can use whatever we have, even if it seems small or insignificant. He used a multitude of individual acts of ministry to let us know that He was with us and He loved us. He kept using our church family to show us His faithfulness and to introduce more bright colors into the tapestry.

That Friday evening, Eric's brother, Nathan, stayed with us at the apartment. When we arrived, we found a basket of fresh blueberry muffins on the table. The sight of my favorite flavor of muffins lifted my spirits. Knowing that someone had taken the time to bake them and leave them nicely arranged for us touched my heart deeply. Their actions were a special gift from God.

Eric, Nathan, and I stayed up talking until midnight. Nathan's presence and loving care was a blessing. His sensitive spirit, shared feeling of loss, keen listening heart and ears, and ability to tackle weighty questions in a thoughtful and compassionate manner was exactly what I needed. I was able to verbalize my lack of understanding of Mom's inability to get the help she needed when she had been so devoted to the Lord and asked Him to lead her to the right doctor and medication. We had prayed that she would get the help she needed, but it never happened.

Nathan brought up the example of Christians in concentration camps in World War II. Some of them died, while others lived. We talked about the Ten Boom family, and how Corrie was spared but her sister died. Both had relied on the Lord and had sought His deliverance. While I still didn't understand why God didn't choose to ensure Mom received the help she needed, I did find comfort in the fact that He alone knew the whole story, and that He could be trusted.

The harsh reality of Mom's suicide required a unique person to minister to me that night. I needed someone with a compassionate heart who was willing to listen, someone who would honestly engage in thoughtful dialogue from a Christian worldview, and who was wise enough to admit that even Christians don't always understand everything. I needed someone to meet me in my pain, help me begin to work through some of it, and in the process would gently point me to Christ.

Nathan wasn't intimidated by my pain. He didn't shy away from it in an attempt to protect himself from the uncomfortable and awkward feelings that often accompany such situations. I was able to express how I felt and what I thought, knowing that Nathan wouldn't run from the conversation or try to shut down feelings and questions from my hurting heart. His sensitive spirit was a channel of blessing to me, and God used him to introduce more bright colors in the cloth.

Chapter 20

Experiencing God's Loving Faithfulness

IN THE DAYS, weeks, and months after Mom's death, we saw God demonstrate His love for us in many ways. My friend, Carol Cassara, gave me a journal to record my thoughts and feelings as I experienced them.

On February 4, 2002, I wrote the following entry.

> *There is so much to write about, and I am not getting time to write. I want to capture it all, but don't feel the time will be available for writing for a while since there is so much to be done. One thing I want to get down is what I'm calling my* Stones of Remembrance. *Just like the children of Israel in olden days used to set up stones as pillars for all to see and remember what great things God did there, so I am setting up mental "stones" of remembrance of God's faithfulness to me during this. He has been so faithful to me thus far, and that gives me the courage, as I look back at what He has already done, to look ahead and know that even though I don't see how I'll ever be able to deal with the pain of her death when it finally sinks in, I take comfort in knowing that God will get me through it one day and one step at a time. I don't have to get through tomorrow or next week until it gets here, and He will be with me through whatever I face. When I remember what He has already done for me, I'm encouraged that He will get me through*

whatever lies ahead. When I get afraid of what the future holds, I mentally run back to the Stones of Remembrance *and hang on to the comfort they bring as they remind me of the faithfulness of God.*

In the Book of Joshua, we find the account of the children of Israel crossing the Jordan River to enter the Promised Land of Canaan. God could have let them cross when the water was at its lowest, but He led them to cross it during the spring flooding season. He wanted there to be no doubt about His supernatural power being used on their behalf. It not only encouraged their faith in Him, but it also served to demonstrate to the nations occupying Canaan that even though Israel wasn't strong, their God was powerful (5:1).

As soon as the priests carrying the ark of the covenant reached the Jordan and their feet touched the water's edge, the water upstream stopped flowing (3:15–16). The priests stood firm on dry ground in the middle of the Jordan while the entire nation of Israel passed by them on dry ground and went to the other side (3:17). Once they were all safely across, the Lord told Joshua to choose twelve men, one from each of the twelve tribes of Israel. They were to go back to where the priests still stood and choose one stone each from the riverbed to be carried on their shoulders to the place where they would camp that night (4:1–5).

That evening they camped at Gilgal on the eastern border of the Jordan River, and Joshua set up the twelve stones. Then he told the people that in the future when their descendants asked their fathers about what the stones meant, they were to tell them about Israel crossing the Jordan on dry ground (4:21–24).

The stones of remembrance were designed to initiate conversations so that the knowledge of God's faithfulness to the older generation would be passed on to the younger generation. We need to do this with our children so they can understand that the living God of the Bible is unchanging and actively involved in lives today.

Memories can be a tremendous encouragement to us in times of trial. As we look back at God's faithfulness to us or others in the past, it gives us courage to go forward, knowing that our faithful God goes with us and will not forsake us.

Psalm 103:2 says, "Praise the LORD, O my soul, and forget not all his benefits." It's especially easy to forget God's benefits during the hard times. Reminders of His previous faithfulness to us encourage us to keep our eyes fixed on Him and on what He wants to do in a situation to bring honor and glory to Himself.

Evidence of God's presence and direction was abundant. God's numerous splashes of bright color stood out all the more boldly because of the dark threads that served as the background for their placement.

The demanding days and many sleepless hours at night ordinarily would have led to a major relapse of my chronic fatigue syndrome and fibromyalgia, but the Lord kept me going.

Normally we didn't even consider a trip to Pennsylvania from New York in January because of poor driving conditions. The Lord gave us traveling mercies not only the weekend of the funeral but also on our biweekly trips through the beginning of June as we took care of settling the estate.

One of the responsibilities I had was to contact the monument company to have them put the date of Mom's death on the tombstone. After they notified me that the work was done, a picture of the tombstone with the year 2001—instead of 2002—on it suddenly came into my mind. It was so clear and came out of nowhere. I had a strong notion that the company had made a mistake and God was preparing me to see it.

The next time we visited the cemetery, Eric initially stayed in the car to give me some time by myself. As I approached the tombstone, I found myself almost expecting to see the wrong year. When I was close enough to read what it said, it was exactly how I had pictured it in my mind. I was humbled that God felt it was important to warn me, and I appreciated Him preparing me to see the incorrect date.

To me, that incident speaks volumes about God's incredible love for me as an individual. I have a feeling that if I completely understood the depth of God's unending love for me, it would change how I live each day.

Over and over, we saw God going before us, smoothing the way and providing for our needs. He provided competent people when special skills were required, compassionate people to help when needed, coordination of many meetings, and the courage and endurance necessary to accomplish all that had to be done.

After our first two trips down, the owners of the apartment we had stayed at closed it up for the rest of the winter. Since we didn't want to take the children to Mom's house yet, I was going to make the next trip by myself. I didn't know how I was going to do alone in the house. I was very thankful when Lin agreed to go with me.

We accomplished a lot that weekend. We cleared out the attic, visited my grandparents, and went to the cemetery. I had one other place to go, and I was glad I had Lin with me.

Jimmy and I had been trying to obtain a copy of the three-and-a-half-page letter Mom had left. I didn't want to go home without it, so I called the state police barracks. The officer in charge of the investigation wasn't in, but I spoke with his supervisor. He listened to my request and asked me some questions. He knew I was going back to Rochester right from the police station, and he asked me who was driving. He wanted to make sure there was someone with me who could drive if necessary. He said he would get a copy of the letter ready for me.

Lin went with me into the station. The officer came out to the lobby with a manila envelope. I was struck by the compassion in his eyes. I wondered how many times he had the responsibility of dealing with survivors of suicide. I felt bad for him having to handle such cases, but I was grateful for the tender yet professional way he dealt with me.

He asked more questions about Mom and the events surrounding her suicide. I answered them and told him some new information that had surfaced since her death. Then he handed me the envelope, and we left.

As soon as we got in the car, I read the letter. It caused a mixture of emotions. When I read that she knew that suicide was not what the Lord wanted as well as not what she wanted, in frustration and sadness I said aloud, "Then why did you do it?" I finished reading the letter, handed it to Lin, and began the long drive home. After Lin silently read the letter, she softly said, "I'm so sorry." I replied, "Me too."

Mom's words stayed in my mind as I drove. I wanted to be able to answer back, to respond, to address what she said, to sit her down and make her understand she wasn't thinking correctly, to instill in her the hope she needed to keep her alive, to assure her that help would be found that would bring lasting relief from the depression and anxiety she had suffered with for so long.

I knew all too well that my final communication with Mom was a one-sided conversation. She got to say what she wanted to say; I wouldn't get to say anything. Our earthly relationship was over. She had chosen to abandon us, just as Dad had done.

How could this have happened to our family? I didn't know. One thing I did know was that I was extremely grateful for Lin's presence. I was also glad to know that God can listen to more than one person at a time, because I was sure she was praying for me the entire time I was talking with my heavenly Father. I'm so thankful He will never abandon me as my earthly parents did.

My journal includes many entries regarding ways I saw God help me. Sometimes I recognized His hand as I watched the tiniest detail perfectly fall into place. Other times, I saw Him at work in much larger matters.

On one of our return visits, Eric's sister, Patti, and her husband, Jim, and their children came to see us when we were at Mom's house. Jim talked about how he felt when his Mom died. It was helpful to hear him give voice to feelings I was experiencing. Having them there and feeling their love was a blessing and a comfort.

The thought of going back to homeschool when I was so foggy and heavy in my head and so tired out was overwhelming. It was something I knew I needed to do, but didn't know how I would pull it off. We missed seven days of school, and then we began again. The Lord helped us get back at it.

My good friend, Sue Terry, invited Daniel to go on some homeschool field trips with her and her boys. They went to the planetarium to see a movie about caves. She took him on a tour of a large grocery store, and he came back the proud owner of a bag of goodies. He also got to see a light show set to patriotic music. Daniel enjoyed each trip, and I was grateful for the break.

Friends in Benton reached out to my brother. It was a relief to know there were people who cared and were checking in on him. Many members of the Benton Volunteer Fire Company were among those who kept tabs on him. I was thankful for each person God used to help Jimmy keep going and not give up on life. It was hard to be so far away from him, especially because he is single. At least I had my husband and children.

A neighboring family went up the driveway daily so it had tire tracks in the snow, rotated which lights were left on inside the house, and kept an eye on the property.

Jimmy and I are still thankful for the many ways people reached out to us.

A couple of my journal entries dealt with my emotional responses to seeing people for the first time after Mom's death. Suicide is an uncomfortable and awkward topic for most people. When Dad died, I hadn't been able to go out in public right away because of being on bed-rest. Now I faced the thought of going to church and wondered how my church family would react when they saw me. I knew they cared and were praying; I just didn't know what our interactions would be like. *Will they talk to me? Will they acknowledge Mom's death was a suicide? Will they avoid me because of their own discomfort with the subject of suicide?* I didn't want them to feel awkward when they saw me. I wanted them to be at ease around me. I also wanted them to be real about what happened and not sidestep the suicide.

The love and support from my church family was wonderful. They took the fact of Mom's suicide in stride and reached out with God's love. Many people expressed their sorrow and their prayer support. Some cried. Many asked about Jimmy. What a blessing it is to be part of the family of God and to feel His love flow through them to us!

The world knows suffering exists. They don't need to see people go through tremendous trials, insisting that they are perfectly peaceful and don't experience any discomfort. They know that isn't real. What they need to see is authentic living that expresses the painful casualties of living in this fallen world and to see God's answer to it being fleshed out in the members of the Body of Christ as they reach out to minister His love and compassion to those in pain. When that happens, others are drawn to our God. They're able to see the sweetness of His Spirit in the actions of His followers.

It's been said that people often forget what others say but seldom forget what they do. I've watched God faithfully and lovingly take our family through many hard times. I remember what my brothers and sisters in Christ did for my family when God used them to minister to us. We experienced His loving care and concern through their actions, and we thank Him—and them—for it.

Chapter 21

Seeing the Other Side of the Tapestry

GOD IS CONTINUALLY at work in our lives in ways that have eternal significance for us and for others. Applying an eternal perspective to life's trials gives those trials a different look than when they are seen only in light of this temporary life.

Our perspective, especially when going through a painful time, is usually focused on the here and now. God's perspective is much larger. His perspective takes today in at a glance and places it properly in its position in His eternal plan.

James 5:8 says, "You too, be patient and stand firm, because the Lord's coming is near."

To me, this life is like a huge tapestry. While on earth, all we see is the bottom side of it with all the blurred colors, threads zigzagging every which way, and knots all over the place. It doesn't make sense, and isn't appealing.

However, on the other side of the tapestry, which we won't see until heaven, God is busy masterfully weaving the colored threads together into a beautiful tapestry of brilliant design with every detail carefully fitted into the picture. Only when we see the tapestry of our life from the other side will we be able to understand what He was designing and what He did with all the dark threads and ugly knots. It makes sense only when viewed from God's perspective.

I have one more story to share with you.

After my third shoulder surgery that I wrote about in an earlier chapter, I had to go for physical therapy at the hospital to gain back the use of my arm and shoulder. One day I was on my back on a table trying to do an exercise that was particularly difficult for me. The room was full of people. Each one had his or her own story of what had brought them to the room that day. There were people there for a range of needs from simple strengthening exercises to learning to walk again.

I was being tested on the exercise, so I was trying to do as many repetitions as I could. It soon became so painful that it was hard to continue.

I told the therapist I didn't think I could keep going. She said something intended to be encouraging, but it didn't have any effect on me. My energy was gone, I was in pain, and I was on the verge of quitting when off to my right I heard someone quietly say, "You can do it." Not knowing who had spoken to me, I turned my head and saw another patient who had stopped what she was doing and was now focused on my plight.

In a matter of moments, an amazing transformation took place in the room. The usual busy sound of equipment being used died out. It was replaced with a stillness that was increasingly punctuated by encouraging comments called out by patients.

I lifted my head slightly and quickly scanned the room from right to left. Everything had stopped. All eyes were on me—patients and therapists alike. Patients called out, "You can do it!" "You're doing great!" "Keep trying!" "Don't give up!"

I laid my head back down and found new strength to continue. With each repetition my faltering attempts began to strengthen into smooth, well-executed motions. The pain was still there, but the cheers of my fellow patients rose up and carried me on to the successful completion of the test.

Afterward, they all turned their attention back to their own individual struggles, but for those few minutes they had focused their attention on someone else's need.

When the therapist had tried to encourage me, it had fallen on deaf ears. Somehow it didn't have much meaning when she said it. However, when those veterans of pain, suffering, and struggling called out to me, it ignited hope and courage in my heart. Their caring and compassionate interest in me changed the outcome of that test. They turned me around from almost quitting to successfully completing it. They also taught me a lesson about life.

When people are going through hard times, they need others to reach out and encourage them. The other patients didn't take the test for me. I had to do it for myself. However, I didn't have to do it *by* myself. Their collective voices of encouragement enabled me to finish well.

That experience serves as a good word picture about how to deal with trials. We all fit into the picture somewhere, depending on what is currently going on in our lives.

Maybe right now you can identify with my plight that day and you are facing something that is painful and draining your strength. If so, don't be ashamed to let people know you're hurting. Ask for help, and don't allow your pride to hinder what God wants to do in ministering His love to you through others.

Maybe you can identify with the patients who called out to me. If so, allow God to use you to reach out and minister His grace to others who are going through trials. Remember that God uses all types and sizes of help to bless people. You might provide a single serving of soup, or maybe it will be an entire meal, dessert included. Maybe it will be something as simple as a hug, an encouraging word, a smile, a short note, or a phone call letting someone know you care.

Or perhaps you can identify most with the therapist, and you know someone is struggling, but you really can't identify with the person in that particular struggle. Or there might be a reason you can't reach out to them in a physical way. If so, you still have a very important part to play in prayer. Some people view prayer as "what one does when he or she isn't able to do anything to 'really' help." The truth is, prayer is the best way you can help someone!

God is the only One who knows the true extent of the good that takes place in a hurting person's life when fellow believers lovingly pray and come alongside the person in a time of need, ministering God's love to them.

After all, like my poster said, "The highest pinnacle of the spiritual life is not happy joy in unbroken sunshine, but absolute and undoubting trust in the love of God." We need to encourage one another to keep choosing to place our trust in God, even when life hurts. Who knows, God may even use us to enable a person to finish this life's race well, instead of quitting.

Hebrews 12:1–2 says, "Therefore, since we are surrounded by such a great cloud of witnesses, let us throw off everything that hinders and the sin that so easily entangles, and let us run with perseverance the race marked out for us. Let us fix our eyes on Jesus, the author and perfecter of our faith, who for the joy set before him endured the cross, scorning its shame, and sat down at the right hand of the throne of God."

For now, while we're still here, we need to keep running this race called life. Let's cheer each other on and help each other up when we stumble and fall.

Keep running! The finish line is just ahead. When we cross it, we'll meet the Master Weaver and get to see the other side of the tapestry.

I can hardly wait!

CPSIA information can be obtained at www.ICGtesting.com
Printed in the USA
BVOW032349300513

322059BV00002B/37/P